JAMES JOYCE

Poems and Shorter Writings

also published by Faber

FINNEGANS WAKE

A SHORTER FINNEGANS WAKE
Edited by Anthony Burgess

ULYSSES: A FACSIMILE OF THE MANUSCRIPT
Introduction by Harry Levin
Preface by Clive Driver

POMES PENYEACH

GIACOMO JOYCE
Introduction by Richard Ellmann

SELECTED LETTERS OF JAMES JOYCE
Edited by Richard Ellmann

JAMES JOYCE
Poems and Shorter Writings

including *Epiphanies, Giacomo Joyce*
and 'A Portrait of the Artist'

EDITED BY RICHARD ELLMANN

A. WALTON LITZ

AND JOHN WHITTIER-FERGUSON

faber and faber

First published in 1991
by Faber and Faber Limited
3 Queen Square London Wcin 3AU

This paperback Edition first published in 2001
Photoset by Wilmaset Birkenhead Wirral
Printed in Italy

The text of *Chamber Music* is included in this
volume by arrangement with Jonathan Cape Limited

A CIP record for this book
is available from the British Library

ISBN 0-571-21098-8

2 4 6 8 10 9 7 5 3 1

Contents

Preface   *page* xiii

PART I – Poems   1

INTRODUCTION   3

CHAMBER MUSIC (1907)   11
I. Strings in the earth and air   13
II. The twilight turns from amethyst   14
III. At that hour when all things have repose   15
IV. When the shy star goes forth in heaven   16
V. Lean out of the window   17
VI. I would in that sweet bosom be   18
VII. My love is in a light attire   19
VIII. Who goes amid the green wood   20
IX. Winds of May, that dance on the sea   21
X. Bright cap and streamers   22
XI. Bid adieu, adieu, adieu   23
XII. What counsel has the hooded moon   24
XIII. Go seek her out all courteously   25
XIV. My dove, my beautiful one   26
XV. From dewy dreams, my soul, arise   27
XVI. O cool is the valley now   28
XVII. Because your voice was at my side   29
XVIII. O Sweetheart, hear you   30
XIX. Be not sad because all men   31
XX. In the dark pine-wood   32
XXI. He who hath glory lost, nor hath   33

XXII. Of that so sweet imprisonment   34
XXIII. This heart that flutters near my heart   35
XXIV. Silently she's combing   36
XXV. Lightly come or lightly go   37
XXVI. Thou leanest to the shell of night   38
XXVII. Though I thy Mithridates were   39
XXVIII. Gentle lady, do not sing   40
XXIX. Dear heart, why will you use me so?   41
XXX. Love came to us in time gone by   42
XXXI. O, it was out by Donnycarney   43
XXXII. Rain has fallen all the day   44
XXXIII. Now, O now, in this brown land   45
XXXIV. Sleep now, O sleep now   46
XXXV. All day I hear the noise of waters   47
XXXVI. I hear an army charging upon the land   48

POMES PENYEACH (1927)   49
1. Tilly   51
2. Watching the Needleboats at San Sabba   52
3. A Flower Given to My Daughter   53
4. She Weeps Over Rahoon   54
5. Tutto è Sciolto   55
6. On the Beach at Fontana   56
7. Simples   57
8. Flood   58
9. Nightpiece   59
10. Alone   60
11. A Memory of the Players in a Mirror at Midnight   61
12. Bahnhofstrasse   62
13. A Prayer   63

ECCE PUER (1932)   65

YOUTHFUL POEMS   69
Et Tu, Healy   71
O fons Bandusiae   71
Are you not weary of ardent ways   72
I only ask you to give me your fair hands   73
La scintille de l'allumette   73
A voice that sings   74
Scalding tears shall not avail   74
Yea, for this love of mine   75
We will leave the village behind   75
Gladly above   75
After the tribulation of dark strife   76
Told sublimely in the language   76
Love that I can give you, lady   77
Wind thine arms round me, woman of
    sorcery   77
Where none murmureth   78
Lord, thou knowest my misery   78
Thunders and sweeps along   79
Though there is no resurrection from the
    past   79
And I have sat amid the turbulent crowd   80
Gorse-flower makes but sorry dining   80
That I am feeble, that my feet   81
The grieving soul. But no grief is thine   81
Let us fling to the winds all moping and
    madness   82
Hands that soothe my burning eyes   82
Now a whisper . . . now a gale   82
O, queen, do on thy cloak   83
'Requiem eternam dona ei, Domine'   83
Of thy dark life, without a love, without a
    friend   84

I intone the high anthem   84
Some are comely and some are sour   85
Flower to flower knits   85
In the soft nightfall   86
Discarded, broken in two   86

POEMS FROM THE *Chamber Music* CYCLE   87
Alas, how sad the lover's lot   89
O, it is cold and still – alas! –   90
She is at peace where she is sleeping   91
I said: I will go down to where   92
Though we are leaving youth behind   93
Come out to where the youth is met   94

THE HOLY OFFICE (1904)   95

GAS FROM A BURNER (1912)   101

OCCASIONAL POEMS   107
  1. G. O'Donnell   109
  2. There was an old lady named Gregory   109
  3. There was a young priest named Delaney   110
  4. There is a weird poet called Russell   110
  5. A holy Hegelian Kettle   110
  6. John Eglinton, my Jo, John   111
  7. Have you heard of the admiral, Togo   111
  8. There once was a Celtic librarian   112
  9. Dear, I am asking a favour   112
 10. O, there are two brothers, the Fays   113
 11. The Sorrow of Love   113
 12. C'era una volta, una bella bambina   114
 13. The flower I gave rejected lies   114
 14. There is a young gallant named Sax   115
 15. There's a monarch who knows no repose   115
 16. Lament for the Yeomen   116

17. There's a donor of lavish largesse   117
18. There is a clean climber called Sykes   117
19. There once was a lounger named Stephen   117
20. Now let awhile my messmates be   118
21. There once was an author named Wells   118
22. Solomon   118
23. D.L.G.   119
24. A Goldschmidt swam in a Kriegsverein   119
25. Dooleysprudence   120
26. There's an anthropoid consul called
    Bennett   122
27. New Tipperary   123
28. To Budgeon, raughty tinker   124
29. A bard once in lakelapt Sirmione   124
30. The Right Heart in the Wrong Place   125
31. The Right Man in the Wrong Place   125
32. O, Mr Poe   126
33. Bis Dat Qui Cito Dat   126
34. And I shall have no peace there for Joyce
    comes more and more   127
35. Who is Sylvia, what is she   127
36. The press and the public misled me   128
37. Jimmy Joyce, Jimmy Joyce, where have
    you been?   128
38. Fréderic's Duck   129
39. I never thought a fountain pen   129
40. Rosy Brook he bought a book   130
41. I saw at Miss Beach's when midday was
    shining   130
42. Bran! Bran! the baker's ban!   130
43. P.J.T.   131
44. Post Ulixem Scriptum   131
45. The clinic was a patched one   133

46. Is it dreadfully necessary 133
47. Rouen is the rainiest place getting 134
48. There's a coughmixture scopolamine 135
49. Troppa Grazia, Sant' Antonio! 135
50. For he's a jolly queer fellow 135
51. Scheveningen, 1927 136
52. Pour Ulysse IX 136
53. Crossing to the Coast 137
54. Hue's Hue? or Dalton's Dilemma 137
55. Buried Alive 138
56. Father O'Ford 138
57. Buy a book in brown paper 139
58. To Mrs H. G. who complained that her visitors kept late hours 139
59. Humptydump Dublin squeaks through his norse 139
60. Stephen's Green 140
61. As I was going to Joyce Saint James' 141
62. Pour la Rime Seulement 142
63. A Portrait of the Artist as an Ancient Mariner 143
64. Pennipomes Twoguineaseach 144
65. There's a genial young poetriarch Euge 145
66. Have you heard of one Humpty Dumpty 145
67. Epilogue to Ibsen's 'Ghosts' 145
68. Goodbye, Zurich, I must leave you 147
69. Le bon repos 148
70. Aiutami dunque, O Musa, nitidissima Calligraphia! 148
71. Come-all-ye 149
72. There's a maevusmarked maggot called Murphy 151

PART II – Shorter Writings   153

EPIPHANIES   155
Introduction   157
Text   161

A PORTRAIT OF THE ARTIST (1904)   201
Introduction   203
Text   211

GIACOMO JOYCE   219
Introduction   221
Text   229

PART III – Notes   243

Abbreviations and References   245
A Note on the Text of the Poems   247
Chamber Music   248
Pomes Penyeach   253
'Ecce Puer'   256
Youthful Poems   257
Poems from the Chamber Music Cycle   259
'The Holy Office'   260
'Gas from a Burner'   261
Occasional Poems   263
Epiphanies   272
'A Portrait of the Artist'   276
Giacomo Joyce   286

Index of Titles and First Lines   295

Preface

When Richard Ellmann died in May 1987 he had not finished this edition of James Joyce's poems and epiphanies. The project was one that he had long cherished, but work on his biography of Oscar Wilde and on the revision of his magisterial *James Joyce* caused inevitable delays. Shortly before his death Dick Ellmann asked me to complete the edition, and this I have been able to do with the invaluable assistance of John Whittier-Ferguson. I also wish to thank Lea Baechler of Columbia University for her careful and intelligent reading of the entire manuscript.

This edition could not have been completed in its present form without the generous assistance of James Joyce's grandson, Stephen J. Joyce. His detailed advice on the arrangement of the volume, and especially on the division into two separate and distinct parts, was invaluable. He improved the edition in many ways by making available to us his unique feeling for and understanding of his grandfather's life and works.

The texts had been established by Ellmann and his research assistants, and we have accepted his editorial decisions – although wherever possible we have checked his transcriptions against the original manuscripts and publications (see the Note on the Text of the Poems). The introductions and notes are our own, with the exception of the introduction to *Giacomo Joyce*, which is based on Ellmann's introduction to the first editions of that work. In making the notes we have drawn freely on Ellmann's *James Joyce*, often adopting his own words. We have also relied heavily on Jacques Aubert's superb edition of Joyce's early writings (*Oeuvres*, Volume

One, Editions Gallimard, Paris, 1982), which is a model of comprehensive and lucid scholarship. Our other debts are acknowledged throughout the notes.

The contents of Joyce's *Collected Poems* – *Chamber Music, Pomes Penyeach*, and 'Ecce Puer' – are presented first, followed by his youthful poems and occasional verses. In addition to the surviving epiphanies, we have included the 1904 'A Portrait of the Artist' and *Giacomo Joyce* because they belong to the same genre of personal meditation, and were – like the epiphanies – rehearsals for the great works to come.

A. Walton Litz

PART I

Poems

Introduction

James Joyce was first and last a poet. His earliest literary effort, at the age of nine, was a poem (of which we have only a fragment) in honour of the dead hero, Charles Stewart Parnell, whose shadow falls over *Dubliners* and *A Portrait of the Artist as a Young Man*. His final achievement was the great poetic tribute to Anna Livia Plurabelle that closes *Finnegans Wake*.

Poetry was Joyce's natural medium for the expression of his most personal sentiments. Beneath their mannered and conventional surfaces, the poems of *Chamber Music* (1907) trace his spiritual progress in the years 1901–4, while the thirteen poems collected in 1927 as *Pomes Penyeach* memorialize 'spots of time' from 1903 to 1924. The first of these, 'Cabra' (later called 'Tilly'), was written shortly after the death of Joyce's mother in August 1903. It takes its title from the location of the Joyce home, 7 St Peter's Terrace, Cabra. In October 1906 Joyce asked if his brother Stanislaus meant him 'to include the Cabra poem' in *Chamber Music*, but the poem was probably too close to his most harrowing experience for publication at that time. Out of key with the tone and subjects of the early lyrics, it is more at home in the autobiographical world of *Pomes Penyeach*.

The heart of *Pomes Penyeach* is a series of poems written in Trieste in 1913–15, at a time when Joyce's art and life were infused with new creative energy. Typical of these is 'She Weeps Over Rahoon', which was composed after Joyce's 1912 visit to the grave of his wife's early sweetheart, Michael Bodkin, the model for Michael Furey in 'The Dead'. The poem gives Joyce's vision of how Nora felt about the living husband

and the dead lover, thus preparing the way for one of the major themes in *Exiles* and *Ulysses*.

Perhaps the most interesting and bizarre episode in the evolution of *Pomes Penyeach* occurred in 1923, when Joyce was drafting the first version of the Tristan and Isolde section in *Finnegans Wake* (11.4). He copied out 'Nightpiece' on the back of a sheet of paper and then surrounded the poem with an introduction and ironic commentary. None of this material reached the final text of *Finnegans Wake*, but it shows that the mature poems strike at the heart of Joyce's secret life. 'Nightpiece' was derived from a dream passage in *Giacomo Joyce* which reflects the inner drama of Joyce's encounter with his Trieste 'lover', Amalia Popper.

Most moving of all the mature poems is 'Ecce Puer' (1932), which was written out of Joyce's despair over the recent death of his father and joy at the birth of his grandson. In 'Ecce Puer' the biblical overtones and ritualized cadences enlarge the short poem into a commentary on the whole course of Joyce's life. It ends:

> A child is sleeping:
> An old man gone.
> O, father forsaken,
> Forgive your son!

When confronted with 'Ecce Puer' and the more successful poems in *Pomes Penyeach*, one might wonder why Joyce turned his poetic impulse into the creation of fiction. The answer lies in the nature of the early poetry and its relationship to the early fiction, especially *Dubliners*.

In the mid-1890s Joyce collected his schoolboy poems under the title *Moods*. Some of these may have been carried over into his next volume, *Shine and Dark* (*c.* 1900). The few verses from *Shine and Dark* that were not lost or destroyed (see pp. 72–86) are highly imitative, derived from the academic romanticism of the 1890s. According to Joyce's brother Stanislaus, the villanelle that Stephen Dedalus composes in Chapter V of *A Portrait of the Artist as a Young Man* was one of these early poems; and we can learn a great deal about Joyce's mature attitude towards his early poetry from his partly ironic treatment of the villanelle in *Portrait*. Although a good example of a familiar 1890s genre, highly accomplished in metric and phrasing, the villanelle – and the pretentious description of the creative process that precedes it – are qualified by being placed in the context of Stephen's precocious aesthetic theories, which strike the reader as more mature and 'original' than the poem.

As Stephen takes his morning walk across the city he repeats to himself 'the song by Ben Jonson which begins: *I was not wearier where I lay*.' If we compare the song from Jonson's *Vision of Delight* with the opening of Stephen's villanelle, the differences are immediately apparent:

> I was not wearier where I lay
> By frozen Tithon's side to-night,
> Than I am willing now to stay,
> And be a part of your delight.
> But I am urged by the Day,
> Against my will, to bid you come away.
>
> Are you not weary of ardent ways,
> Lure of the fallen seraphim?
> Tell no more of enchanted days.

By contrasting Jonson's controlled lines with Stephen's imitative, *fin-de-siècle* weariness, Joyce has subtly criticized his hero and provided us with some acute commentary on *Shine and Dark*.

Most of the poems in *Chamber Music* were written between 1901 and 1904, although the volume was not published until 1907. Yeats viewed these poems as the work of 'a young man who is practising his instrument, taking pleasure in the mere handling of the stops', and this is certainly the dominant impression conveyed by *Chamber Music*. There are obvious debts to the Romantic poets (XXVI), and some poems suggest the mood poetry of the 1890s (especially II, which dates from the *Shine and Dark* period). Some of the verses are fine imitations of the Elizabethan lyric (VI); others are modelled on the Irish folk song (XXXI). Joyce was an excellent singer who loved Elizabethan music, and it was his hope – later fulfilled – that the poems of *Chamber Music* would be set to music by 'someone who knows old English music such as I like'. He thought of *Chamber Music* as a 'suite' of songs, and the collection is filled with musical imagery. More importantly, the songs are held together by a rhythmical structure of leitmotivs and recurrent themes. There is a pervasive debt to Verlaine, whose 'Art poétique' – with its emphasis on musical form and the nuance – stands behind the whole collection.

But it would be a mistake to think of *Chamber Music* solely in terms of imitated styles. There are occasions when Joyce, like the Elizabethan sonneteers, uses the conventions for new effects. One such occasion is Poem XII. According to Stanislaus Joyce, this lyric grew out of an experience his brother had one evening in 1904. A young girl whom James admired remarked that the pale, mist-encircled moon looked 'tearful'. James replied that it 'looks to me like the chubby hooded face of some jolly fat Capuchin'. After the girl had left, Joyce 'tore open a cigarette-box and standing under a street lamp wrote the two verses of the song on the inside of the box'.

In Poem XII the argument against sentimentality and the 'pathetic fallacy' is conducted through a deliberate clash of styles. The girl sees the moon as a conventional emblem of Love's sad mysteries, and her view is expressed in an appropriately pathetic language. But Joyce, in the manner of Jules Laforgue, converts the 'hooded moon' of convention into the startling image of a 'comedian Capuchin', thus deflating the sentimentality of 'Love in ancient plenilune'. This deliberate interplay of styles is not common in *Chamber Music* – Joyce is more often a prisoner of the forms he imitates – but it is important as a sign of his growing command of language and his deep-felt need for a manner of writing that could combine irony with lyricism.

Another atypical poem that demands attention is XXXVI, 'I hear an army'. In this lyric Joyce adopted a style found in Yeats's more intense poems of the 1890s – such as 'The Valley of the Black Pig' – and made it his own. The emphasis is entirely on sound, not sight – 'hear', 'thunder', 'cry', 'moan', 'clanging', 'shouting' – yet the total impact of the poem is that of a powerful visual image. As the poem develops, the scene struggles into sight like the army out of the sea; the materials of nightmare have been given precise expression. It is not surprising that when Ezra Pound published his *Des Imagistes* anthology in 1914 he included 'I hear an army' and praised it for its 'objective' form. Long before the Imagist movement came into being, Joyce had broken his own bondage to the 1890s and achieved a condensed, energetic style of his own. Poems such as 'I hear an army' prepared the way for *Dubliners*, just as Imagism helped prepare the reading public for the economic style of Joyce's stories.

And yet, in spite of his successes in *Chamber Music*, Joyce reacted violently against the work. By 1906 he was referring to it contemptuously as a 'young man's book', and wishing that he could find another title which would 'to a certain extent repudiate the book, without altogether disparaging it'. In 1907 he nearly cancelled publication, explaining: 'All that kind of thing is false'. How can we account for this change in attitude? One answer, probably the most important one, is that Joyce was by temperament a sentimentalist, and that this sentimentality was too easily exposed in the revelations of unmediated lyric poetry. *Chamber Music* always loomed large in Joyce's emotional life, especially in his relationship with Nora (after a reconciliation in 1909 Joyce sent her a parchment copy of *Chamber Music*, with her initials and his entwined on the cover, accompanied by a sentimental letter). But in his art Joyce was determined to control his sentimentality, and to accomplish this aim he needed the greater objectivity – the ironic contexts – provided by fiction. When Joyce told his brother in 1906 that 'a page of *A Little Cloud* gives me more pleasure than all my verses', he was clearly thinking of the stricter control found in the later stories of *Dubliners*. That balance of sympathy and detachment, of sentiment and irony, which is the signature of his mature art could be attained only fitfully in the forms of *Chamber Music*.

Another aspect of *Chamber Music* that indicates the direction of Joyce's development is the collection's general design. As the songs accumulated, Joyce made several tentative arrangements of them, the last and most important being an arrangement of the first thirty-four songs which dates from 1905. However, by late 1906 he was so indifferent to the fate of the volume that he allowed his brother Stanislaus to determine the published sequence. Stanislaus gave the thirty-six songs a musical sequence, hoping 'to suggest a closed episode of youth and love', and Joyce accepted this without comment. But the earlier arrangement of thirty-four songs was obviously still in his mind when he wrote in 1909 to an Irish composer who was setting some of the poems to music: 'The central song is XIV after which the movement is all downwards

[8]

until XXXIV which is vitally the end of the book. XXXV and XXXVI are tailpieces just as I and III are preludes.'

In addition to *Chamber Music* and *Pomes Penyeach* Joyce wrote a number of occasional poems, many of them comic or satiric in nature. After 'Ecce Puer' the most significant are *The Holy Office* (1904), his angry diatribe against the Ireland that he believed had driven him into exile; and *Gas from a Burner* (1912), a savage broadside prompted by his abortive 1912 trip to Dublin. Background information on these and the other occasional poems will be found in the notes, along with further information about the texts and various arrangements of *Chamber Music* and *Pomes Penyeach*.

A.W.L.

CHAMBER MUSIC

1907

I

Strings in the earth and air
   Make music sweet;
Strings by the river where
   The willows meet.

There's music along the river
   For Love wanders there,
Pale flowers on his mantle,
   Dark leaves on his hair.

All softly playing,
   With head to the music bent,
And fingers straying
   Upon an instrument.

The twilight turns from amethyst
    To deep and deeper blue,
The lamp fills with a pale green glow
    The trees of the avenue.

The old piano plays an air,
    Sedate and slow and gay;
She bends upon the yellow keys,
    Her head inclines this way.

Shy thoughts and grave wide eyes and hands
    That wander as they list —
The twilight turns to darker blue
    With lights of amethyst.

III

At that hour when all things have repose,
   O lonely watcher of the skies,
   Do you hear the night wind and the sighs
Of harps playing unto Love to unclose
   The pale gates of sunrise?

When all things repose do you alone
   Awake to hear the sweet harps play
   To Love before him on his way,
And the night wind answering in antiphon
   Till night is overgone?

Play on, invisible harps, unto Love,
   Whose way in heaven is aglow
   At that hour when soft lights come and go,
Soft sweet music in the air above
   And in the earth below.

When the shy star goes forth in heaven
   All maidenly, disconsolate,
Hear you amid the drowsy even
   One who is singing by your gate.
His song is softer than the dew
   And he is come to visit you.

O bend no more in revery
   When he at eventide is calling,
Nor muse: Who may this singer be
   Whose song about my heart is falling?
Know you by this, the lover's chant,
   'Tis I that am your visitant.

V

Lean out of the window,
   Goldenhair,
I heard you singing
   A merry air.

My book was closed;
   I read no more,
Watching the fire dance
   On the floor.

I have left my book,
   I have left my room,
For I heard you singing
   Through the gloom.

Singing and singing
   A merry air,
Lean out of the window,
   Goldenhair.

I would in that sweet bosom be
  (O sweet it is and fair it is!)
Where no rude wind might visit me.
  Because of sad austerities
I would in that sweet bosom be.

I would be ever in that heart
  (O soft I knock and soft entreat her!)
Where only peace might be my part.
  Austerities were all the sweeter
So I were ever in that heart.

VII

My love is in a light attire
    Among the apple-trees,
Where the gay winds do most desire
    To run in companies.

There, where the gay winds stay to woo
    The young leaves as they pass,
My love goes slowly, bending to
    Her shadow on the grass;

And where the sky's a pale blue cup
    Over the laughing land,
My love goes lightly, holding up
    Her dress with dainty hand.

VIII

Who goes amid the green wood
  With springtide all adorning her?
Who goes amid the merry green wood
  To make it merrier?

Who passes in the sunlight
  By ways that know the light footfall?
Who passes in the sweet sunlight
  With mien so virginal?

The ways of all the woodland
  Gleam with a soft and golden fire —
For whom does all the sunny woodland
  Carry so brave attire?

O, it is for my true love
  The woods their rich apparel wear —
O, it is for my own true love,
  That is so young and fair.

IX

Winds of May, that dance on the sea,
Dancing a ring-around in glee
From furrow to furrow, while overhead
The foam flies up to be garlanded,
In silvery arches spanning the air,
Saw you my true love anywhere?
       Welladay! Welladay!
       For the winds of May!
Love is unhappy when love is away!

X

Bright cap and streamers,
  He sings in the hollow:
  Come follow, come follow,
    All you that love.
Leave dreams to the dreamers
  That will not after,
  That song and laughter
    Do nothing move.

With ribbons streaming
  He sings the bolder;
  In troop at his shoulder
    The wild bees hum.
And the time of dreaming
  Dreams is over —
  As lover to lover,
    Sweetheart, I come.

Bid adieu, adieu, adieu,
   Bid adieu to girlish days,
Happy Love is come to woo
   Thee and woo thy girlish ways —
The zone that doth become thee fair,
The snood upon thy yellow hair.

When thou hast heard his name upon
   The bugles of the cherubim
Begin thou softly to unzone
   Thy girlish bosom unto him
And softly to undo the snood
That is the sign of maidenhood.

XII

What counsel has the hooded moon
　　Put in thy heart, my shyly sweet,
Of Love in ancient plenilune,
　　Glory and stars beneath his feet —
A sage that is but kith and kin
With the comedian Capuchin?

Believe me rather that am wise
　　In disregard of the divine,
A glory kindles in those eyes
　　Trembles to starlight. Mine, O Mine!
No more be tears in moon or mist
For thee, sweet sentimentalist.

XIII

Go seek her out all courteously,
  And say I come,
Wind of spices whose song is ever
  Epithalamium.
O, hurry over the dark lands
  And run upon the sea
For seas and lands shall not divide us,
  My love and me.

Now, wind, of your good courtesy
  I pray you go,
And come into her little garden
  And sing at her window;
Singing: The bridal wind is blowing
  For Love is at his noon;
And soon will your true love be with you,
  Soon, O soon.

My dove, my beautiful one,
  Arise, arise!
  The night-dew lies
Upon my lips and eyes.

The odorous winds are weaving
  A music of sighs:
  Arise, arise,
My dove, my beautiful one!

I wait by the cedar tree,
  My sister, my love.
  White breast of the dove,
My breast shall be your bed.

The pale dew lies
  Like a veil on my head.
  My fair one, my fair dove,
Arise, arise!

From dewy dreams, my soul, arise,
    From love's deep slumber and from death,
For lo! the trees are full of sighs
    Whose leaves the morn admonisheth.

Eastward the gradual dawn prevails
    Where softly-burning fires appear,
Making to tremble all those veils
    Of grey and golden gossamer.

While sweetly, gently, secretly,
    The flowery bells of morn are stirred
And the wise choirs of faery
    Begin (innumerous!) to be heard.

XVI

O cool is the valley now
    And there, love, will we go
For many a choir is singing now
    Where Love did sometime go.
And hear you not the thrushes calling,
    Calling us away?
O cool and pleasant is the valley
    And there, love, will we stay.

XVII

Because your voice was at my side
  I gave him pain,
Because within my hand I held
  Your hand again.

There is no word nor any sign
  Can make amend –
He is a stranger to me now
  Who was my friend.

XVIII

O Sweetheart, hear you
    Your lover's tale;
A man shall have sorrow
    When friends him fail.

For he shall know then
    Friends be untrue
And a little ashes
    Their words come to.

But one unto him
    Will softly move
And softly woo him
    In ways of love.

His hand is under
    Her smooth round breast;
So he who has sorrow
    Shall have rest.

XIX

Be not sad because all men
   Prefer a lying clamour before you:
Sweetheart, be at peace again –
   Can they dishonour you?

They are sadder than all tears;
   Their lives ascend as a continual sigh.
Proudly answer to their tears:
   As they deny, deny.

XX

In the dark pine-wood
  I would we lay,
In deep cool shadow
  At noon of day.

How sweet to lie there,
  Sweet to kiss,
Where the great pine-forest
  Enaisled is!

Thy kiss descending
  Sweeter were
With a soft tumult
  Of thy hair.

O, unto the pine-wood
  At noon of day
Come with me now,
  Sweet love, away.

XXI

He who hath glory lost, nor hath
   Found any soul to fellow his,
Among his foes in scorn and wrath
   Holding to ancient nobleness,
That high unconsortable one –
His love is his companion.

XXII

Of that so sweet imprisonment
  My soul, dearest, is fain —
Soft arms that woo me to relent
  And woo me to detain.
Ah, could they ever hold me there
Gladly were I a prisoner!

Dearest, through interwoven arms
  By love made tremulous,
That night allures me where alarms
  Nowise may trouble us;
But sleep to dreamier sleep be wed
Where soul with soul lies prisoned.

XXIII

This heart that flutters near my heart
  My hope and all my riches is,
Unhappy when we draw apart
  And happy between kiss and kiss;
My hope and all my riches — yes! —
And all my happiness.

For there, as in some mossy nest
  The wrens will divers treasures keep,
I laid those treasures I possessed
  Ere that mine eyes had learned to weep.
Shall we not be as wise as they
Though love live but a day?

XXIV

Silently she's combing,
   Combing her long hair,
Silently and graciously,
   With many a pretty air.

The sun is in the willow leaves
   And on the dappled grass,
And still she's combing her long hair
   Before the looking-glass.

I pray you, cease to comb out,
   Comb out your long hair,
For I have heard of witchery
   Under a pretty air,

That makes as one thing to the lover
   Staying and going hence,
All fair, with many a pretty air
   And many a negligence.

XXV

Lightly come or lightly go:
   Though thy heart presage thee woe,
Vales and many a wasted sun,
   Oread let thy laughter run
Till the irreverent mountain air
Ripple all thy flying hair.

Lightly, lightly – ever so:
   Clouds that wrap the vales below
At the hour of evenstar
   Lowliest attendants are;
Love and laughter song-confessed
When the heart is heaviest.

XXVI

Thou leanest to the shell of night,
  Dear lady, a divining ear.
In that soft choiring of delight
  What sound hath made thy heart to fear?
Seemed it of rivers rushing forth
From the grey deserts of the north?

  That mood of thine, O timorous,
Is his, if thou but scan it well,
  Who a mad tale bequeaths to us
At ghosting hour conjurable –
  And all for some strange name he read
  In Purchas or in Holinshed.

XXVII

Though I thy Mithridates were,
　Framed to defy the poison-dart,
Yet must thou fold me unaware
　To know the rapture of thy heart,
And I but render and confess
The malice of thy tenderness.

For elegant and antique phrase,
　Dearest, my lips wax all too wise;
Nor have I known a love whose praise
　Our piping poets solemnize,
Neither a love where may not be
Ever so little falsity.

XXVIII

Gentle lady, do not sing
   Sad songs about the end of love;
Lay aside sadness and sing
   How love that passes is enough.

Sing about the long deep sleep
   Of lovers that are dead, and how
In the grave all love shall sleep:
   Love is aweary now.

XXIX

Dear heart, why will you use me so?
   Dear eyes that gently me upbraid,
Still are you beautiful – but O,
   How is your beauty raimented!

Through the clear mirror of your eyes,
   Through the soft sigh of kiss to kiss,
Desolate winds assail with cries
   The shadowy garden where love is.

And soon shall love dissolved be
   When over us the wild winds blow –
But you, dear love, too dear to me,
   Alas! why will you use me so?

XXX

Love came to us in time gone by
  When one at twilight shyly played
And one in fear was standing nigh –
  For Love at first is all afraid.

We were grave lovers. Love is past
  That had his sweet hours many a one;
Welcome to us now at the last
  The ways that we shall go upon.

XXXI

O, it was out by Donnycarney
   When the bat flew from tree to tree
My love and I did walk together;
   And sweet were the words she said to me.

Along with us the summer wind
   Went murmuring – O, happily! –
But softer than the breath of summer
   Was the kiss she gave to me.

XXXII

Rain has fallen all the day.
   O come among the laden trees:
The leaves lie thick upon the way
   Of memories.

Staying a little by the way
   Of memories shall we depart.
Come, my beloved, where I may
   Speak to your heart.

XXXIII

Now, O now, in this brown land
   Where Love did so sweet music make
We two shall wander, hand in hand,
   Forbearing for old friendship' sake,
Nor grieve because our love was gay
Which now is ended in this way.

A rogue in red and yellow dress
   Is knocking, knocking at the tree;
And all around our loneliness
   The wind is whistling merrily.
The leaves – they do not sigh at all
When the year takes them in the fall.

Now, O now, we hear no more
   The villanelle and roundelay!
Yet will we kiss, sweetheart, before
   We take sad leave at close of day.
Grieve not, sweetheart, for anything –
The year, the year is gathering.

XXXIV

Sleep now, O sleep now,
    O you unquiet heart!
A voice crying 'Sleep now'
    Is heard in my heart.

The voice of the winter
    Is heard at the door.
O sleep, for the winter
    Is crying 'Sleep no more.'

My kiss will give peace now
    And quiet to your heart –
Sleep on in peace now,
    O you unquiet heart!

XXXV

All day I hear the noise of waters
    Making moan,
Sad as the sea-bird is, when going
    Forth alone,
He hears the winds cry to the waters'
    Monotone.

The grey winds, the cold winds are blowing
    Where I go.
I hear the noise of many waters
    Far below.
All day, all night, I hear them flowing
    To and fro.

I hear an army charging upon the land,
　And the thunder of horses plunging, foam about their
　　knees:
Arrogant, in black armour, behind them stand,
　Disdaining the reins, with fluttering whips, the
　　charioteers.

They cry unto the night their battle-name:
　I moan in sleep when I hear afar their whirling laughter.
They cleave the gloom of dreams, a blinding flame,
　Clanging, clanging upon the heart as upon an anvil.

They come shaking in triumph their long, green hair:
　They come out of the sea and run shouting by the shore.
My heart, have you no wisdom thus to despair?
　My love, my love, my love, why have you left me alone?

POMES PENYEACH

1927

Tilly

He travels after a winter sun,
Urging the cattle along a cold red road,
Calling to them, a voice they know,
He drives his beasts above Cabra.

The voice tells them home is warm.
They moo and make brute music with their hoofs.
He drives them with a flowering branch before him,
Smoke pluming their foreheads.

Boor, bond of the herd,
Tonight stretch full by the fire!
I bleed by the black stream
For my torn bough!

Dublin, 1904

Watching the Needleboats at San Sabba

I heard their young hearts crying
Loveward above the glancing oar
And heard the prairie grasses sighing:
No more, return no more!

O hearts, O sighing grasses,
Vainly your loveblown bannerets mourn!
No more will the wild wind that passes
Return, no more return.

Trieste, 1912

A Flower Given to My Daughter

Frail the white rose and frail are
Her hands that gave
Whose soul is sere and paler
Than time's wan wave.

Rosefrail and fair — yet frailest
A wonder wild
In gentle eyes thou veilest,
My blueveined child.

Trieste, 1913

She Weeps Over Rahoon

Rain on Rahoon falls softly, softly falling,
Where my dark lover lies.
Sad is his voice that calls me, sadly calling,
At grey moonrise.

Love, hear thou
How soft, how sad his voice is ever calling,
Ever unanswered, and the dark rain falling,
Then as now.

Dark too our hearts, O love, shall lie and cold
As his sad heart has lain
Under the moongrey nettles, the black mould
And muttering rain.

Trieste, 1913

5

Tutto è Sciolto

A birdless heaven, seadusk, one lone star
Piercing the west,
As thou, fond heart, love's time, so faint, so far,
Rememberest.

The clear young eyes' soft look, the candid brow,
The fragrant hair,
Falling as through the silence falleth now
Dusk of the air.

Why then, remembering those shy
Sweet lures, repine
When the dear love she yielded with a sigh
Was all but thine?

Trieste, 1914

On the Beach at Fontana

Wind whines and whines the shingle,
The crazy pierstakes groan;
A senile sea numbers each single
Slimesilvered stone.

From whining wind and colder
Grey sea I wrap him warm
And touch his trembling fineboned shoulder
And boyish arm.

Around us fear, descending
Darkness of fear above
And in my heart how deep unending
Ache of love!

Trieste, 1914

Simples

O bella bionda,
Sei come l'onda!

Of cool sweet dew and radiance mild
The moon a web of silence weaves
In the still garden where a child
Gathers the simple salad leaves.

A moondew stars her hanging hair
And moonlight kisses her young brow
And, gathering, she sings an air:
Fair as the wave is, fair, art thou!

Be mine, I pray, a waxen ear
To shield me from her childish croon
And mine a shielded heart for her
Who gathers simples of the moon.

Trieste, 1915

8

Flood

Goldbrown upon the sated flood
The rockvine clusters lift and sway,
Vast wings above the lambent waters brood
Of sullen day.

A waste of waters ruthlessly
Sways and uplifts its weedy mane
Where brooding day stares down upon the sea
In dull disdain.

Uplift and sway, O golden vine,
Your clustered fruits to love's full flood,
Lambent and vast and ruthless as is thine
Incertitude!

Trieste, 1915

Nightpiece

Gaunt in gloom,
The pale stars their torches,
Enshrouded, wave.
Ghostfires from heaven's far verges faint illume,
Arches on soaring arches,
Night's sindark nave.

Seraphim,
The lost hosts awaken
To service till
In moonless gloom each lapses muted, dim.
Raised when she has and shaken
Her thurible.

And long and loud,
To night's nave upsoaring,
A starknell tolls
As the bleak incense surges, cloud on cloud,
Voidward from the adoring
Waste of souls.

Trieste, 1915

Alone

The moon's greygolden meshes make
All night a veil,
The shorelamps in the sleeping lake
Laburnum tendrils trail.

The sly reeds whisper to the night
A name – her name –
And all my soul is a delight,
A swoon of shame.

Zurich, 1916

A Memory of the Players in a Mirror at Midnight

They mouth love's language. Gnash
The thirteen teeth
Your lean jaws grin with. Lash
Your itch and quailing, nude greed of the flesh.
Love's breath in you is stale, worded or sung,
As sour as cat's breath,
Harsh of tongue.

This grey that stares
Lies not, stark skin and bone.
Leave greasy lips their kissing. None
Will choose her what you see to mouth upon.
Dire hunger holds his hour.
Pluck forth your heart, saltblood, a fruit of tears,
Pluck and devour!

Zurich, 1917

Bahnhofstrasse

The eyes that mock me sign the way
Whereto I pass at eve of day,

Grey way whose violet signals are
The trysting and the twining star.

Ah star of evil! star of pain!
Highhearted youth comes not again

Nor old heart's wisdom yet to know
The signs that mock me as I go.

Zurich, 1918

13

A Prayer

Again!
Come, give, yield all your strength to me!
From far a low word breathes on the breaking brain
Its cruel calm, submission's misery,
Gentling her awe as to a soul predestined.
Cease, silent love! My doom!

Blind me with your dark nearness, O have mercy,
    beloved enemy of my will!
I dare not withstand the cold touch that I dread.
Draw from me still
My slow life! Bend deeper on me, threatening head,
Proud by my downfall, remembering, pitying
Him who is, him who was!

Again!
Together, folded by the night, they lay on earth. I hear
From far her low word breathe on my breaking brain.
Come! I yield. Bend deeper upon me! I am here.
Subduer, do not leave me! Only joy, only anguish,
Take me, save me, soothe me, O spare me!

Paris, 1924

ECCE PUER

1932

Ecce Puer

Of the dark past
A child is born.
With joy and grief
My heart is torn.

Calm in his cradle
The living lies.
May love and mercy
Unclose his eyes!

Young life is breathed
On the glass;
The world that was not
Comes to pass.

A child is sleeping:
An old man gone.
O, father forsaken,
Forgive your son!

YOUTHFUL POEMS

[Breaks in the manuscript texts of the poems
are indicated by rows of dashes:
see the note on page 257]

Et Tu, Healy

My cot alas that dear old shady home
Where oft in youthful sport I played
Upon thy verdant grassy fields all day
Or lingered for a moment in thy bosom shade.

— — — — —

His quaint-perched aerie on the crags of Time
Where the rude din of this . . . century
Can trouble him no more.

O fons Bandusiae

Brighter than glass Bandusian spring
    For mellow wine and flowers meet,
The morrow thee a kid shall bring
    Boding of rivalry and sweet
Love in his swelling horns. In vain
He, wanton offspring, deep shall stain
Thy clear cold streams with crimson rain.

The raging dog star's season thou,
    Still safe from in the heat of day,
When oxen weary of the plough
    Yieldst thankful cool for herds that stray.
Be of the noble founts! I sing
The oak tree o'er thine echoing
Crags, thy waters murmuring.

Are you not weary of ardent ways,
Lure of the fallen seraphim?
Tell no more of enchanted days.

Your eyes have set man's heart ablaze
And you have had your will of him.
Are you not weary of ardent ways?

Above the flame the smoke of praise
Goes up from ocean rim to rim.
Tell no more of enchanted days.

Our broken cries and mournful lays
Rise in one eucharistic hymn.
Are you not weary of ardent ways?

While sacrificing hands upraise
The chalice flowing to the brim,
Tell no more of enchanted days.

And still you hold our longing gaze
With languorous look and lavish limb!
Are you not weary of ardent ways?
Tell no more of enchanted days.

I only ask you to give me your fair hands.
Ah, dearest, this one grace, it will be the last.
How fast are they fled, halcyon days, how fast.
Nor you nor I can arrest time's running sands.
Enough that we have known the pleasure of love
Albeit pleasure, fraught with an heartfelt grief.
Though our love season hath been marvellous
Yet we have loved and told our passion – [ending.]
Then fade the uncertain day and come the night.

La scintille de l'allumette
Qui se cachait entre vos mains
A ensorcelé ma cigarette –
Ah, l'étoile de l'allumette!

Il me plait bien d'observer

– – – – –

A voice that sings
Like viol strings
  Through the wane
Of the pale year
Lulleth me here
  With its strain.

My soul is faint
At the bell's plaint,
  Ringing deep;
I think upon
A day bygone
  And I weep.

Away! Away!
I must obey
  This drear wind,
Like a dead leaf
In aimless grief
  Drifting blind.

– – – – –

Scalding tears shall not avail,
Love shall be to us for aye
    An heart-breaking tale.

Ah, how fast your warm heart beats –
Fluttering upon my breast.
Lay aside your deep unrest;
We have eaten all the sweets;
The golden fruit falls from the tree

– – – – –

Yea, for this love of mine
I have given all I had;
For she was passing fair,
And I was passing mad.

All flesh, it is said,
Shall wither as the grass;
The fuel for the oven
Shall be consumed, alas!

We will leave the village behind,
Merrily, you and I,
Tramp it smart and sing to the wind,
With the Rommany Rye.

– – – – –

Gladly above,
The lover listens
In deepest love.

– – – – –

After the tribulation of dark strife,
And all the ills of the earth, crying for my release.

Why is the truth so hidden and the land of dreams so far,
That the feet of the climber fail on the upward way;
Although in the purple distance burns a red-gold star,
There are briers on the mountain and the weary feet have bled.
    The homesteads and the fireglow bid him stay:
And the burden of his body is like a burden of lead.

– – – – –

Told sublimely in the language
Which the shining angels knew.
Tearless choirs of joyful servants,
Sounding cymbals, brazen shawms,
Distant hymns of myriad planets,
Heavenly maze of full-voiced psalms.
Only, when the heart is peaceful,
When the soul is moved to love,
May we hearken to those voices
Starry singing from above.

– – – – –

Love that I can give you, lady
Ah, that they haven't, lady
        Lady witchin', lady mine.

O, you say that I torment you
        With my verses, lady mine
Faith! the best I had I sent you,
        Don't be laughin', lady mine.
I am foolish to be hopin'
That you left your window open,

– – – – –

– – – – –

. . . Wind thine arms round me, woman of sorcery,
While the lascivious music murmurs afar:
I will close mine eyes, and dream as I dance with thee,
And pass away from the world where my sorrows are.

Faster and faster! strike the harps in the hall!
Woman, I fear that this dance is the dance of death!
Faster! – ah, I am faint . . . and, ah, I fall.
The distant music mournfully murmureth.

– – – – –

Where none murmureth,
Let all grieving cease
     And fade as a breath,
And come the final peace
     Which men call death.

Joy and sorrow
     Pass away and be fled,
Welcome the morrow

– – – – –

Lord, thou knowest my misery,
See the gifts which I have brought,
Sunshine on a dying face
Stricken flowers, seldom sought.

See the pale moon, the sunless dawn
Of my fainting feebleness;
But only shed thy dew on me
And I shall teem in fruitfulness.

– – – – –

Thunders and sweeps along
The roadway. The rain is strong
And the tide of it lays all pain.

I am in no idle passion
That my threadbare coat is torn,
And quaint of fashion.
My humour is devil-may-care,
As the labourer's song upborne
On the quiet air.

– – – – –

Though there is no resurrection from the past,
It matters not, for one pure thing I see,
On which no stain, no shadow has been cast.

I see the image of my love unclouded,
Like a white maiden in some hidden place,
In a bright cloak, woven of my hopes, enshrouded,
And looking at me with a smiling face.

I do not care for an honourable mention

– – – – –

And I have sat amid the turbulent crowd,
And have assisted at their boisterous play;
I have unbent myself and shouted loud,
And been as blatant and as coarse as they.

I have consorted with vulgarity
And am indelibly marked with its fell kiss,
Meanly I lived upon casual charity
Eagerly drinking of the dregs of bliss.

— — — — —

— Gorse-flower makes but sorry dining,
Mulberries make no winecups full,
Grass-threads lacing and entwining
Weave no linen by the waters —
Said the mother to her daughters.
The sisters viewed themselves reclining,
Heeding not, undutiful.
The first girl wished for spinning,
And she asked a spindle of gold;
The second sister wished to weave,

— — — — —

— — — — —

That I am feeble, that my feet
Are weak as young twigs in the wind;

That this poor heart, which was of old
So reckless, passionate and proud,
Shivers at trifles and wanes cold
Whene'er thy fair face shows a cloud.

A golden bird in azure skies,
Late radiant with sunbright wings,
Is fallen down to earth, and sighs

— — — — —

— — — — —

The grieving soul. But no grief is thine
Who driftest the creeks and shallows among,
Shaking thy hair of the clinging brine.
Why is thy garment closer drawn?
Thine eyes are sad, my sorrowful one,
Thy tresses are strewn with the woe of dawn,
The pearly dawn weeping the sun.
Hast thou no word – to raise – to ease
Our souls? Well, go, for the faint far cry
Of the seabirds calls thee over the seas.

Let us fling to the winds all moping and madness,
Play us a jig in the spirit of gladness
On the creaky, old squeaky strings of the fiddle.

The why of the world is an answerless riddle
Puzzlesome, tiresome, hard to unriddle
To the seventeen devils with sapient sadness:
                                     Tra la, tra la.

— — — — —

        Hands that soothe my burning eyes
        In the silence of moonrise,
        At the midmost hour of night,
                         Trouble me not.

        Fingers soft as rain alight,
        Like flowers borne upon the night
        From the pure deeps of sapphire skies.

— — — — —

        Now a whisper . . . now a gale
        List, ah list, how drear it calls!

        There is in it that appals
        As it wanders round the walls,
        Like a forlorn woman, pale.
                         List the wind!

O, queen, do on thy cloak
Of scarlet, passion hue,
And lift, attending folk,
A mournful ululu,
For flame-spun is the cloak.

. . . . . .

Fling out thy voice, O lyre,
Forth of thy seven strings.

– – – – –

'Requiem eternam dona ei, Domine';
Silently, sorrowfully I bent down my head,
For I had hated him – a poor creature of clay:
And all my envious, bitter, cruel thoughts that came
Out of the past and stood by the bier whereon he lay
Pointed their long, lean fingers through the gloom . . . O Name
Ineffable, proud Name to whom the cries ascend
From lost, angelical orders, seraph flame to flame,
For this end have I hated him – for this poor end?

– – – – –

Of thy dark life, without a love, without a friend,
  Here is, indeed, an end.

There are no lips to kiss this foul remains of thee,
  O, dead Unchastity!
The curse of loneliness broods silent on thee still,
  Doing its utmost will,
And men shall cast thee justly to thy narrow tomb,
  A sad and bitter doom.

– – – – –

I intone the high anthem,
Partaking in their festival.
Swing out, swing in, the night is dark,
Magical hair, alive with glee,
Winnowing spark after spark,
Star after star, rapturously.
Toss and toss, amazing arms;
Witches, weave upon the floor
Your subtle-woven web of charms.

– – – – –

Some are comely and some are sour,
Some are dark as wintry mould,
Some are fair as a golden shower.
To music liquid as a stream
They move with dazzling symmetry;
Their flashing limbs blend in a gleam
Of luminous-swift harmony.
They wear gold crescents on their heads,
Hornèd and brilliant as the moon:

– – – – –

– – – – –

Flower to flower knits
Of willing lips and leaves:
Thy springtide of bliss
Maketh the breezes sing,
And blossoms yield their kiss
Unto amorous thieves.

But the arrow that flies
Must fall spent at last;

– – – – –

In the soft nightfall
Hear thy lover call,
Hearken the guitar!
Lady, lady fair
Snatch a cloak in haste,
Let thy lover taste
The sweetness of thy hair.

– – – – –

– – – – –

Discarded, broken in two.

Sing to mine ear, O rain,
Thine ultimate melody;
That the dearest loss is gain
In a holier treasury;

That a passionate cry in the night
For a woman, hidden and pale,

– – – – –

POEMS FROM THE
Chamber Music
CYCLE

Alas, how sad the lover's lot
Whose love to him can do offence!
Alas, that beauty should have not
Stability nor reverence!

My heart is taken in a net
Misled ill-used made captive too
By promises and shows – but yet
Happy with vows that are untrue.

Poor heart, alas, that such offence
Love all too reverent may not chide,
That winds that have no reverence
Abide where love doth still abide!

O, it is cold and still – alas! –
The soft white bosom of my love,
Wherein no mood of guile or fear
But only gentleness did move.
She heard, as standing on the shore,
A bell above the waters toll,
She heard the call of 'Come away'
Which is the calling of the soul

They covered her with linen white
And set white candles at her head
And loosened out her glorious hair
And laid her on a snow-white bed.
I saw her passing like a cloud,
Discreet and silent and apart.
O, little joy and great sorrow
Is all the music of the heart

The fiddle has a mournful sound
That's playing in the street below.
I would I lay with her I love –
And who is here to say me no?
We lie upon the bed of love
And lie together in the ground:
To live, to love and to forget
Is all the wisdom lovers have.

She is at peace where she is sleeping,
Her pale hands folded on her shroud,
And I am wandering in the world
Alone and sorrowful and proud.
She heard, as standing on the shore,
A bell above the waters toll,
She heard the call of 'Come away'
Which is the calling of the soul.

They covered her with linen white
And laid her on a snow-white bed
And loosened out her glorious hair
And set white candles at her head.
I remember her moving of old
Amid grave days as one apart.
O, little joy and great sorrow
Is all the music of my heart.

The fiddle has a mournful sound
That's playing in the street below –
I would I lay with her I love:
And who is there to say me no?
I would I lay in the dark earth
For sorrow bids me now depart
And the remembering of love
Makes a sad music in my heart.

I said: I will go down to where
She waits amid the silences,
And look upon her face and smile;
And she will cover me with her hair.
I shall forget what sorrow is
And rest with her a little while.

I put aside sorrow and care
For these may not be where she is,
For these are enemies. I came
And sought the glimmer of her hair
Amid the desolate silences
And cried upon the gloom her name.

Though we are leaving youth behind
And ways of pleasure would reprove
Thou hast engraven in the mind
Thy name, O many-weathered love

And should the grace, the presence – all
That was thy magic – cease to be,
Here in the bosom ever shall
Endure thy dear charactery.

Come out to where the youth is met
Under the moon, beside the sea,
And leave your weapon and your net,
Your loom and your embroidery.

Bring back the pleasantness of days
And crystal moonlight on the shore.
Your feet have woven many a maze
In old times on the ivory floor.

The weapons and the looms are mute
And feet are hurrying by the sea.
I hear the viol and the flute,
The sackbut and the psaltery.

THE HOLY OFFICE
1904

The Holy Office

Myself unto myself will give
This name Katharsis-Purgative.
I, who dishevelled ways forsook
To hold the poets' grammar-book,
Bringing to tavern and to brothel
The mind of witty Aristotle,
Lest bards in the attempt should err
Must here be my interpreter:
Wherefore receive now from my lip
Peripatetic scholarship.   10
To enter heaven, travel hell,
Be piteous or terrible
One positively needs the ease,
Of plenary indulgences.
For every true-born mysticist
A Dante is, unprejudiced,
Who safe at ingle-nook, by proxy,
Hazards extremes of heterodoxy
Like him who finds a joy at table,
Pondering the uncomfortable.   20
Ruling one's life by common sense
How can one fail to be intense?
But I must not accounted be
One of that mumming company –
With him who hies him to appease
His giddy dames' frivolities
While they console him when he whinges
With gold-embroidered Celtic fringes –
Or him who sober all the day
Mixes a naggin in his play –   30

Or him whose conduct 'seems to own',
His preference for a man of 'tone' —
Or him who plays the rugged patch
To millionaires in Hazelhatch
But weeping after holy fast
Confesses all his pagan past —
Or him who will his hat unfix
Neither to malt nor crucifix
But show to all that poor-dressed be
His high Castilian courtesy —
Or him who loves his Master dear —
Or him who drinks his pint in fear —
Or him who once when snug abed
Saw Jesus Christ without his head
And tried so hard to win for us
The long-lost works of Eschylus.
But all these men of whom I speak
Make me the sewer of their clique.
That they may dream their dreamy dreams
I carry off their filthy streams
For I can do those things for them
Through which I lost my diadem,
Those things for which Grandmother Church
Left me severely in the lurch.
Thus I relieve their timid arses,
Perform my office of Katharsis.
My scarlet leaves them white as wool
Through me they purge a bellyful.
To sister mummers one and all
I act as vicar-general
And for each maiden, shy and nervous,
I do a similar kind service.
For I detect without surprise

That shadowy beauty in her eyes,
The 'dare not' of sweet maidenhood
That answers my corruptive 'would'.
Whenever publicly we meet
She never seems to think of it;
At night when close in bed she lies
And feels my hand between her thighs   70
My little love in light attire
Knows the soft flame that is desire.
But Mammon places under ban
The uses of Leviathan
And that high spirit ever wars
On Mammon's countless servitors
Nor can they ever be exempt
From his taxation of contempt.
So distantly I turn to view
The shamblings of that motley crew,   80
Those souls that hate the strength that mine has
Steeled in the school of old Aquinas.
Where they have crouched and crawled and prayed
I stand the self-doomed, unafraid,
Unfellowed, friendless and alone,
Indifferent as the herring-bone,
Firm as the mountain-ridges where
I flash my antlers on the air.
Let them continue as is meet
To adequate the balance-sheet.   90
Though they may labour to the grave
My spirit shall they never have
Nor make my soul with theirs at one
Till the Mahamanvantara be done:
And though they spurn me from their door
My soul shall spurn them evermore.

GAS FROM A BURNER

1912

Gas from a Burner

Ladies and gents, you are here assembled
To hear why earth and heaven trembled
Because of the black and sinister arts
Of an Irish writer in foreign parts.
He sent me a book ten years ago.
I read it a hundred times or so,
Backwards and forwards, down and up,
Through both the ends of a telescope.
I printed it all to the very last word
But by the mercy of the Lord   10
The darkness of my mind was rent
And I saw the writer's foul intent.
But I owe a duty to Ireland:
I hold her honour in my hand,
This lovely land that always sent
Her writers and artists to banishment
And in a spirit of Irish fun
Betrayed her own leaders, one by one.
'Twas Irish humour, wet and dry,
Flung quicklime into Parnell's eye;   20
'Tis Irish brains that save from doom
The leaky barge of the Bishop of Rome
For everyone knows the Pope can't belch
Without the consent of Billy Walsh.
O Ireland my first and only love
Where Christ and Caesar are hand and glove!
O lovely land where the shamrock grows!
(Allow me, ladies, to blow my nose)
To show you for strictures I don't care a button
I printed the poems of Mountainy Mutton   30

And a play he wrote (you've read it, I'm sure)
Where they talk of 'bastard', 'bugger' and 'whore'
And a play on the Word and Holy Paul
And some woman's legs that I can't recall
Written by Moore, a genuine gent
That lives on his property's ten per cent:
I printed mystical books in dozens:
I printed the table book of Cousins
Though (asking your pardon) as for the verse
'Twould give you a heartburn on your arse:
I printed folklore from North and South
By Gregory of the Golden Mouth:
I printed poets, sad, silly and solemn:
I printed Patrick What-do-you-Colm:
I printed the great John Milicent Synge
Who soars above on an angel's wing
In the playboy shift that he pinched as swag
From Maunsel's manager's travelling-bag.
But I draw the line at that bloody fellow,
That was over here dressed in Austrian yellow,
Spouting Italian by the hour
To O'Leary Curtis and John Wyse Power
And writing of Dublin, dirty and dear,
In a manner no blackamoor printer could bear.
Shite and onions! Do you think I'll print
The name of the Wellington Monument,
Sydney Parade and the Sandymount tram,
Downes's cakeshop and Williams's jam?
I'm damned if I do — I'm damned to blazes!
Talk about *Irish Names of Places*!
It's a wonder to me, upon my soul,
He forgot to mention Curly's Hole.
No, ladies, my press shall have no share in
So gross a libel on Stepmother Erin.

I pity the poor – that's why I took
A red-headed Scotchman to keep my book.
Poor sister Scotland! Her doom is fell;
She cannot find any more Stuarts to sell.
My conscience is fine as Chinese silk:
My heart is as soft as buttermilk.   70
Colm can tell you I made a rebate
Of one hundred pounds on the estimate
I gave him for his Irish Review.
I love my country – by herrings I do!
I wish you could see what tears I weep
When I think of the emigrant train and ship.
That's why I publish far and wide
My quite illegible railway guide.
In the porch of my printing institute
The poor and deserving prostitute   80
Plays every night at catch-as-catch-can
With her tight-breeched British artilleryman
And the foreigner learns the gift of the gab
From the drunken draggletail Dublin drab.
Who was it said: Resist not evil?
I'll burn that book, so help me devil.
I'll sing a psalm as I watch it burn
And the ashes I'll keep in a one-handled urn.
I'll penance do with farts and groans
Kneeling upon my marrowbones.   90
This very next lent I will unbare
My penitent buttocks to the air
And sobbing beside my printing press
My awful sin I will confess.
My Irish foreman from Bannockburn
Shall dip his right hand in the urn
And sign crisscross with reverent thumb
Memento homo upon my bum.

[105]

OCCASIONAL POEMS

1

G. O'Donnell

Poor little Georgie, the son of a lackey,
Famous for 'murphies', spirits, and 'baccy
Renowned all around for a feathery head
Which had a tendency to become red.
His genius was such that all men used to stare,
His appearance was that of a bull at a fair.
The pride of Kilmainham, the joy of the class,
A moony, a loony, an idiot, an ass.
Drumcondra's production, and by the same rule,
The prince of all pot-boys, a regular fool.
All hail to the beauteous, the lovely, all hail
And hail to his residence in Portland gaol.

2

There was an old lady named Gregory
Who said: 'Come, all ye poets in beggary.'
But she found her imprudence
When hundreds of students
Cried: 'We're in that noble category.'

3

There was a young priest named Delaney
Who said to the girls, '*Nota bene*,
  'Twould tempt the archbishop
  The way that you swish up
Your skirts when the weather is rainy.'

4

There is a weird poet called Russell
Who wouldn't eat even a mussel
When chased by an oyster
He ran to a cloister
Away from the beef and the bustle.

The cloister he called the 'Hermetic'
I found it a fine diuretic
A most energetic
And mental emetic
Heretic, prophetic, ascetic.

5

A holy Hegelian Kettle
Has faith which we cannot unsettle
If no one abused it
He might have reduced it
But now he is quite on his mettle.

John Eglinton, my Jo, John,
When last had you a   ?
I fear ye canna go, John,
Although ye are na spent.
O   begin to fel', John,
Ye canna mak' it flow,
And even if it swell, John
The lassies wadna know.

John Eglinton, my Jo, John,
I dinna like to say
Of course ye must have sinned, John
When ye were young and gay
It canna be remorse, John,
That keeps ye fra a ride
Your virtue is a farce, John,
Ye cardna if ye tried

Have you heard of the admiral, Togo,
Who said to the girls, 'It is no go;
        But when we come back,
        Then each jolly Jack –
Yókogó! Yókogó! Yókogó!'

8

There once was a Celtic librarian
Whose essays were voted Spencerian,
    His name is Magee
    But it seems that to me
He's a flavour that's more Presbyterian.

9

Dear, I am asking a favour
    Little enough
This, that thou shouldst entype me
    This powdery puff

I had no heart for your troubling,
    Dearest, did I
Only possess a typewriter or
    Money to buy

Thine image, dear, rosily litten
    Ever shall be
Thereafter that thou hast typewritten
    These things for me —

10

O, there are two brothers, the Fays,
Who are excellent players of plays,
    And, needless to mention, all
    Most unconventional,
Filling the world with amaze.

But I angered these brothers, the Fays,
Whose ways are conventional ways,
    For I lay in my urine
    While ladies so pure in
White petticoats ravished my gaze.

11

The Sorrow of Love

If any told the blue ones that
    mountain-footed move,
They would bend down and with batons,
    belabour my love.

12

C'era una volta, una bella bambina
Che si chiamava Lucia
Dormiva durante il giorno
Dormiva durante la notte
Perché non sapeva camminare
Perché non sapeva camminare
Dormiva durante il giorno
Dormiva durante la notte.

13

The flower I gave rejected lies.
Sad is my lot for all to see.
Humiliation burns my eyes.
The Grace of God abandons me.

As Alberic sweet love forswore
The power of cursed gold to wield
So you, who lust for metal ore,
Forswear me for a copperfield.

Rejoice not yet in false bravado
The pimpernel you flung away
Shall torchlike burn your El Dorado.
Vengeance is mine. I will repay.

There is a young gallant named Sax
Who is prone to hayfever attacks
　　For the prime of the year
　　To Cupid so dear
Stretches maidens – and men! – on their backs.

There's a monarch who knows no repose
For he's dressed in a dual trunk hose
　　And ever there itches
　　Some part of his breeches;
How he stands it the Lord only knows.

Lament for the Yeomen

(from the German of Felix Beran)

And now is come the war, the war:
And now is come the war, the war:
And now is come the war, the war.
War! War!

For soldiers are they gone now:
For soldiers all.
Soldiers and soldiers!
All! All!

Soldiers must die, must die.
Soldiers all must die.
Soldiers and soldiers and soldiers
Must die.

What man is there to kiss now,
To kiss, to kiss,
O white soft body, this
Thy soft sweet whiteness?

17

There's a donor of lavish largesse
Who once bought a play in MS
      He found out what it all meant
      By the final instalment
But poor Scriptor was left in a mess.

18

There is a clean climber called Sykes
Who goes scrambling o'er ditches and dikes,
      To skate on his scalp
      Down the side of an alp
Is the kind of diversion he likes.

19

There once was a lounger named Stephen
Whose youth was most odd and uneven.
      He throve on the smell
      Of a horrible hell
That a Hottentot wouldn't believe in.

20

Letter to Ezra
Pound July 1917

Now let awhile my messmates be
My ponderous Penelope
And my Ulysses born anew
In Dublin as an Irish jew.
With them I'll sit, with them I'll drink
Nor heed what press and pressmen think
Nor leave their rockbound house of joy
For Helen or for windy Troy.

21

There once was an author named Wells
Who wrote about science, not smells [. . .]
The result is a series of cells.

22

Solomon

There's a hairyfaced Moslem named Simon
Whose tones are not those of a shy man
     When with cast iron lungs
     He howls twentyfive tongues —
But he's not at all easy to rhyme on.

23

D. L. G.

There's a George of the Georges named David
With whose words we are now night and day fed
    He cries: I'll give small rations
    To all the small nations.
Bully God made this world – but I'll save it.

24

A Goldschmidt swam in a Kriegsverein
As wise little Goldschmidts do,
And he loved every scion of the Habsburg line,
Each Archduke proud, the whole jimbang crowd,
And he felt that they loved him, too.
Herr Rosenbaum and Rosenfeld
And every other Feld except Schlachtfeld
All worked like niggers, totting rows of crazy figures,
To save Kaiser Karl and Goldschmidt, too.

Chorus:
For he said it is bet-bet-better
To stick stamps on some God-damned letter
    Than be shot in a trench
    Amid shells and stench,
Jesus Gott, Donnerwet-wet-wetter.

25

Dooleysprudence

(*Air: Mr. Dooley*)

Who is the man when all the gallant nations run to war
Goes home to have his dinner by the very first cablecar
And as he eats his cantaloups contorts himself in mirth
To read the blatant bulletins of the rulers of the earth?
    It's Mr. Dooley,
    Mr. Dooley,
    The coolest chap our country ever knew
    'They are out to collar
    The dime and dollar'
    Says Mr. Dooley-ooley-ooley-oo.

Who is the funny fellow who declines to go to church
Since pope and priest and parson left the poor man in the
    lurch
And taught their flocks the only way to save all human souls
Was piercing human bodies through with dumdum
    bulletholes?
    It's Mr. Dooley,
    Mr. Dooley,
    The mildest man our country ever knew
    'Who will release us
    From Jingo Jesus?'
    Prays Mr. Dooley-ooley-ooley-oo.

Who is the meek philosopher who doesn't care a damn
About the yellow peril or problem of Siam
And disbelieves that British Tar is water from life's fount
And will not gulp the gospel of the German on the Mount?
>It's Mr. Dooley,
>Mr. Dooley,
>The broadest brain our country ever knew
>'The curse of Moses
>On both your houses'
>Cries Mr. Dooley-ooley-ooley-oo.

Who is the cheerful imbecile who lights his long chibouk
With pages of the pendect, penal code and Doomsday Book
And wonders why bald justices are bound by law to wear
A toga and a wig made out of someone else's hair?
>It's Mr. Dooley,
>Mr. Dooley,
>The finest fool our country ever knew
>'They took that toilette
>From Pontius Pilate,
>Thinks Mr. Dooley-ooley-ooley-oo.

Who is the man who says he'll go the whole and perfect hog
Before he pays an income tax or licence for a dog
And when he licks a postagestamp regards with smiling
>scorn
The face of king or emperor or snout of unicorn?
>It's Mr. Dooley,
>Mr. Dooley,
>The wildest wag our country ever knew
>'O my poor tummy
>His backside gummy!'
>Moans Mr. Dooley-ooley-ooley-oo.

Who is the tranquil gentleman who won't salute the State
Or serve Nabuchodonosor or proletariat
But thinks that every son of man has quite enough to do
To paddle down the stream of life his personal canoe?
        It's Mr. Dooley,
        Mr. Dooley,
        The wisest lad our country ever knew
        'Poor Europe ambles
        Like sheep to shambles!'
        Sighs Mr. Dooley-ooley-ooley-oo.

Who is the sunny sceptic who fights shy of Noah's arks
When they are made in Germany by Engels and by Marx
But when the social deluge comes and rain begins to pour
Takes off his coat and trousers and prepares to swim
    ashore?
        It's Mr. Dooley,
        Mr. Dooley,
        The bravest boy our country ever knew
        With arms akimbo
        'I'll find that rainbow!'
        Shouts Mr. Dooley-ooley-ooley-oo.

26

    There's an anthropoid consul called Bennett,
    With the jowl of a jackass or jennet,
        He must muzzle or mask it
        In the waste paper basket,
    When he rises to bray in the Senate.

New Tipperary

Up to rheumy Zurich came an Irishman one day
As the town was rather dull he thought he'd give a play
So that German propagandists might be rightly riled
But the bully British philistine once more made Oscar wild.
　　　For the C. G. is not literary
　　　And his handymen are rogues
　　　Our C. G.'s about as literary
　　　As an Irish kish of brogues.
　　　We paid all expenses,
　　　As the good Swiss public knows,
　　　But we'll be damn well damned before we pay for
　　　Private Carr's swank hose.

When the play was over Carr with rage began to dance,
Howling 'I wanta twenty quid for them there dandy pants:
Fork us out the tin or comrade Bennett here and me,
We're going to wring your bloody necks. We're out for
　　　liberty.'
　　　Chorus (as above)

They found a Norse solicitor to prove that white was black,
That one can boss in Switzerland beneath the Union Jack,
They marched to the Gerichtshof but came down like Jack
　　　and Jill,
While the pants came tumbling after . . . and the judge is
　　　laughing still.

No, the C. G. is not literairy
And his handymen are rogues,
Our C. G.'s about as literairy
As an Irish kish of brogues.
Goodbye, brother Bennett!
Goodbye, chummy Carr!
If you put a beggar upon horseback,
Why, 'e dunno where 'e are!

28

To Budgeon, raughty tinker

Oh! Budgeon, boozer, bard, and canvas dauber
If to thine eyes these lines should sometime come
Bethink thee that the fleshpots of old Egypt
Nothing avail if beauty's heart would beat.
Wherefore forswear butter besmeared Ravioli
Which do the mainsprings of thy talent clog
On Roggenbrot, in Joghurt, and cold water,
Paint and be damned. We wait. Begin, and end.

29

A bard once in lakelapt Sirmione
Lived in peace, eating locusts and honey
    Till a son of a bitch
    Left him dry on the beach
Without clothes, boots, time, quiet or money.

The Right Heart in the Wrong Place

Of spinach and gammon
Bull's full to the crupper,
White lice and black famine
Are the mayor of Cork's supper.
But the pride of old Ireland
Must be damnably humbled
If a Joyce is found cleaning
The boots of a Rumbold

S.O.S.

The Right Man in the Wrong Place

(*Air: My heart's in my highlands*)

The pig's in the barley,
The fat's in the fire:
Old Europe can hardly
Find twopence to buy her.
Jack Spratt's in his office,
Puffed, powdered and curled:
Rumbold's in Warsaw —
All's right with the world!

O, Mr Poe,
You're very slow!
St Monsieur Valette
Il nous faut la galette!
So haste to ease us
For the love of Jesus!
Kreutzbomben,
Sakrament!

33

Bis Dat Qui Cito Dat

Yanks who hae wi' Wallace read,
Yanks whom Joyce has often bled,
Welcome to the hard plank bed,
    And bolschevistic flea.
Who for Bloom and Inisfail
Longs to pine in Sing Sing jail,
Picking oakum without bail,
    Let him publish me.

34

And I shall have no peace there for Joyce comes more and
    more,
Dropping from a tramp or a taxi to where the white wine
    swills.
Then midnight's all of a shimmy and Bloom a bloody bore
And morning full – of bills! bills! bills!

35

Who is Sylvia, what is she
That all our scribes commend her?
Yankee, young and brave is she
The west this grace did lend her,
That all books might published be.

Is she rich as she is brave
For wealth oft daring misses?
Throngs about her rant and rave
To subscribe for *Ulysses*
But, having signed, they ponder grave.

Then to Sylvia let us sing
Her daring lies in selling.
She can sell each mortal thing
That's boring, beyond telling.
To her let us buyers bring.

            J. J.
            after
            W. S.

36

The press and the public misled me
So brand it as slander and lies
That I am the bloke with the watches
And that you are the chap with the ties.

37

— Jimmy Joyce, Jimmy Joyce, where have you been?
— I've been to London to see the queen —
— Jimmy Joyce, Jimmy Joyce, what saw you, tell?
— I saw a brass bed in the Euston Hotel.

Fréderic's Duck

(air: Dougherty's Duck)

Cantus Plenus
Now Wallace he heard that Fréderic's was the dearest place
    to dine
So he took the Joyces there to have combustible duck and
    wine.
The toothpicks cost a pound apiece, the salt a guinea a
    grain:
When Wallace saw the bill he felt an epigastric pain.

Chorus Coenatorum
Fréderic, Fréderic, Fréderic, O! My word, you pile it on!
A tour of the world is cheaper than a meal in the *Tour
    d'Argent*.
I'd rather eat hot dog in the street or dine for half a buck
Than sweat in full dress in your poultry-press and be bled
    like Fréderic's duck.

39

I never thought a fountain pen
Exemption gave as well as solace.
If critics blame my style again
I'll say 'twas given me by Wallace.

Shem the Penman

Rosy Brook he bought a book
Though he didn't know how to spell it.
Such is the lure of literature
To the lad who can buy it and sell it.

I saw at Miss Beach's when midday was shining
A bard with fresh water drone drowsily on
I came when Miss Beach was distant and dining
The bard was asleep but the water was gone.

(with apologies to Thomas Moore)

Bran! Bran! the baker's ban!
Gobble it quick and die if you can.
Forgive us this day our deadly bread
But give us old Kellogg's bran poultice instead.

P. J. T.

There's a funny facepainter dubbed Tuohy
Whose bleaklook is rosybud bluey
    For when he feels strong
    He feels *your* daub's all wrong
But when he feels weak he feels wooey.

Post Ulixem Scriptum

(*Air: Molly Brannigan*)

Man dear, did you never hear of buxom Molly Bloom at all,
As plump an Irish beauty, Sir, as any Levi-Blumenthal?
If she sat in the viceregal box Tim Healy'd have no room at all,
    But curl up in a corner at a glance from her eye.
The tale of her ups and downs would aisy fill a handybook
That would cover the two worlds at once from Gibraltar
    'cross to Sandy Hook.
But now that tale is told, ochone, I've lost my daring dandy
    look:
    Since Molly Bloom has left me here alone for to cry.

Man dear, I remember when my roving time was troubling
    me
We picknicked fine in storm or shine in France and Spain
    and Hungary
And she said I'd be her first and last while the wine I poured
    went bubbling free
        Now every male you meet with has a finger in her
    pie.
Man dear, I remember with all the heart and brain of me
I arrayed her for the bridal but, O, she proved the bane of
    me.
With more puppies sniffing round her than the wooers of
    Penelope
        She's left me on her doorstep like a dog for to die.

My left eye is wake and his neighbour full of water, man.
I cannot see the lass I limned as Ireland's gamest Daughter,
    man,
When I hear her lovers tumbling in their thousands for to
    court her, man,
        If I was sure I'd not be seen I'd sit down and cry.
May you live, may you love like this gaily spinning earth of
    ours,
And every morn a gallant sun awake you with new wealth
    of gold
But if I cling like a child to the clouds that are your
    petticoats
        O Molly, handsome Molly, sure you won't let me
    die!

45

The clinic was a patched one
Its outside old as rust
And every stick beneath that roof
Lay four foot thick in dust.

46

Is it dreadfully necessary
      AND
(I mean that I pose etc) is it useful, I ask
this
          Heat!?
We all know Mercury will
      when
he Kan!
    but as Dante saith:
    1 Inferno is enough
Basta, he said, *un' inferno, perbacco*!
And that bird –
    Well!
He
—

—

—
    oughter know!

—

—

—

(with apologies to Mr Ezra Pound)

Rouen is the rainiest place getting
Inside all impermeables, wetting
Damp marrow in drenched bones.
Midwinter soused us coming over Le Mans
Our inn at Niort was the Grape of Burgundy
But the winepress of the Lord thundered over that grape of
    Burgundy
And we left it in a hurgundy.
(Hurry up, Joyce, it's time!)

I heard mosquitoes swarm in old Bordeaux
So many!
I had not thought the earth contained so many
(Hurry up, Joyce, it's time)

Mr Anthologos, the local gardener,
Greycapped, with politeness full of cunning
Has made wine these fifty years
And told me in his southern French
Le petit vin is the surest drink to buy
For if 'tis bad
Vous ne l'avez pas payé
(Hurry up, hurry up, now, now, now!)

But we shall have great times,
When we return to Clinic, that waste land
O Esculapios!
(Shan't we? Shan't we? Shan't we?)

48

There's a coughmixture scopolamine
And its equal has never been seen
  'Twould make staid Tutankamen
  Laugh and leap like a salmon
And his mummy hop Skotch on the green.

49

Troppa Grazia, Sant' Antonio!

 E. P. is fond of an extra inch
 Whenever the 'ell it's found.
 But wasn't J. J. the son of a binch
 To send him an extra pound?

50

 For he's a jolly queer fellow
 And I'm a jolly queer fellow
 And Roth's bad German for yellow
 Which nobody can deny

Scheveningen, 1927

Sáy, ain't thís succéss fool aúthor
Jést a dándy páradóx,
Wíth that sílvier béach behínd him,
Hówling: Hélp! I'm ón the rócks!

à H. W.

Pour Ulysse IX

L. B. lugubriously still treads the press of pain
But J. J.'s joyicity is on the jig again
And he'll highkick every abelboobied humballoon he cain
   As he goes jubiling along.

Souvenir de la Chandeleur 1928
Paris

          jokes
These capital letters represent the dancer
kicking the balloons of imposture into the
heaven of deception.

53

Crossing to the Coast

(*Air: Killaloo*)

Don't talk of Congo Stanley
Or Livingstone the manly
Or the boys walked marching, parching
    from Atlanta to the sea.

When I lift me left lad lazy,
Begor, I take it aisy.
Dijon – Lyon – par Avignon –
It's long toulong for me!

J'y. J'y.
(suis le reste)

54

Hue's Hue?
or Dalton's Dilemma

What colour's Jew Joyce when he's rude and grim both,
Varied virid from groening and rufous with rage
And if this allrotter's allred as a roth
Can he still blush unirish yet green as a gage?

55

Buried Alive

Now have I fed and eaten up the rose
Which then she laid within my stiffcold hand.
That I should ever feed upon a rose
I never had believed in liveman's land.

Only I wonder was it white or red
The flower that in this dark my food has been.
Give us, and if Thou give, thy daily bread,
Deliver us from evil, Lord. Amen.

56

Father O'Ford

(*Air: Father O'Flynn*)

O Father O'Ford you've a masterful way with you.
Maid, wife and widow are wild to make hay with you.
Blonde and brunette turn-about run away with you.
You've such a way with you, Father O'Ford.

That instant they see the sunshine from your eyes
Their hearts flitter flutter, they think and they sigh:
We kiss ground before thee, we madly adore thee
And crave and implore thee to take us, O Lord!

57

Buy a book in brown paper
From Faber and Faber
To see Annie Liffey trip, tumble and caper.
Sevensinns in her singthings,
Plurabells on her prose,
Seashell ebb music wayriver she flows.

58

To Mrs H. G. who complained that her visitors kept late hours

Go ca'canny with the cognac
And of the Wine fight shy,
Keep your eye upon the hourglass
That leaves the beaker dry.

Guestfriendliness to callers
Is your surest thief of time,
They're so much at holmes when with you
They don't dream of gugging heim.

59

Humptydump Dublin squeaks through his norse,
Humptydump Dublin hath a horriple vorse,
    And, with all his kinks english
    Plus his irishmanx brogues,
Humpydump Dublin's grandada of rogues.

Stephen's Green

The wind stood up and gave
   a shout.
He whistled on his fingers
   and

Kicked the withered leaves
   about
And thumped the branches
   with his hand

And said he'd kill and kill
   and kill,
And so he will and so he
   will.

Der Wind stand auf, liess
   los einen Schrei,
Pfiff mit den Fingern schrill
   dabei.

Wirbelte dürres Laub durch
   den Wald
Und hämmerte Äste mit
   Riesengewalt.

Zum Tod, heult, zum Tod
   und Mord!
Und meint es ernst : ein
   Wind, ein Wort.

Les Verts de Jacques

Le vent d'un saut lance son
   cri,
Se siffle sur les doigts et puis

Trépigne les feuilles
   d'automne,
Craque les branches qu'il
   assomme.

Je tuerai, crie-t-il, holà!

Et vous verrez s'il le fera!

Surgit Boreas digitorum

Fistulam, faciens et
   clamorem.

Pes pugno certat par
   (oremus!)
Foliis quatit omne nemus.

Caedam, ait, caedam,
   caedam!
Nos ne habeat ille praedam.

Vinden staar op med en vild Huru,	*Balza in piè Fra Vento e grida.*
Han piber paa fingerne og nu	*Tre dita in bocca fischia la sfida.*
Sparker bladenes flyvende flok.	*Tira calci, pesta botte:*
Traeerne troer han er Ragnarok	*Ridda di foglie e frasche rotte.*
Skovens liv og blod vil han draebe og drikke.	*Ammazzerò, ei urla, O gente!*
Hvad der bliver at goere, det ved ieg ikke.	*E domeneddio costui non mente diuraddio*

61

As I was going to Joyce Saint James'
I met with seven extravagant dames;
Every dame had a bee in her bonnet,
With bats from the belfry roosting upon it.
And Ah, I said, poor Joyce Saint James,
What can he do with these terrible dames?
Poor Saint James Joyce.

62

Pour la Rime Seulement

À Pierre de Lanux
dit Valery Larbaud
prête moi un dux
qui peut conduire l'assault
mes pioux piou sont fondus
et meurent de malaise
sois ton petit tondu
pour la gloire d'Ares
Lanux de la Pierre
à Beaulard fit réplique
foute-moi la guerre
avec tes soldiques
car pour l'Italie
presto fais tes malles
tire ta bonne partie
avec quelques balles
à ces mots Leryval
file en obobus
et comme le vieux Hannibal
perce le blocus
à peine atterre sa mine
qu'on crie à la foire
un sous la Mursoline
pour l'arrats de gloire

A Portrait of the Artist as an Ancient Mariner

I met with an ancient scribelleer
As I scoured the pirates' sea
His sailes were alullt at nought coma null
Not raise the wind could he.

The bann of Bull, the sign of Sam
Burned crimson on his brow.
And I rocked at the rig of his bricabrac brig
With K.O. 11 on his prow

Shakefears & Coy danced poor old joy
And some of their steps were corkers
As they shook the last shekels like phantom freckels
His pearls that had poisom porkers

The gnome Norbert read rich bills of fare
The ghosts of his deep debauches
But there was no bibber to slip that scribber
The price of a box of matches

For all cried, Schuft! He has lost the Luft
That made his U.boat go
And what a weird leer wore that scribelleer
As his wan eye winked with woe.

He dreamed of the goldest sands uprolled
By the silviest Beach of Beaches
And to watch it dwindle gave him Kugelkopfschwindel
Till his eyeboules bust their stitches

His hold shipped seas with a drunkard's ease
And its deadweight grew and grew
While the witless wag still waived his flag
Jemmyrend's white and partir's blue.

His tongue stuck out with a dragon's drouth
For a sluice of schweppes and brandy
And but for the glows on his roseate nose
Youd have staked your goat he was Gandhi.

For the Yanks and Japs had made off with his traps!
So that stripped to the stern he clung
While, increase of a cross, an Albatross
Abaft his nape was hung.

64

Pennipomes Twoguineaseach

Sing a song of shillings
A guinea cannot buy,
Thirteen tiny pomikins
Bobbing in a pie.

The printer's pie was published
And the pomes began to sing
And wasn't Herbert Hughesius
As happy as a king!

65

There's a genial young poetriarch Euge
Who hollers with heartiness huge:
    Let sick souls sob for solace
    So the *jeunes* joy with Jolas!
Book your berths! *Après mot, le déluge.*

66

Have you heard of one Humpty Dumpty
How he fell with a roll and a rumble
And lay low like Low All of a crumple
    By the butt of the Magazine's Wall?

67

Epilogue to Ibsen's 'Ghosts'

Dear quick, whose conscience buried deep
The grim old grouser has been salving,
Permit one spectre more to peep.
I am the ghost of Captain Alving.

Silenced and smothered by my past
Like the lewd knight in dirty linen
I struggle forth to swell the cast
And air a long-suppressed opinion.

For muddling weddings into wakes
No fool could vie with Parson Manders.
I, though a dab at ducks and drakes,
Let gooseys serve or sauce their ganders.

My spouse bore me a blighted boy,
Our slavey pupped a bouncing bitch.
Paternity, thy name is joy
When the wise sire knows which is which.

Both swear I am that selfsame man
By whom their infants were begotten.
Explain, fate, if you care and can
Why one is sound and one is rotten.

Olaf may plod his stony path
And live as chastely as Susanna
Yet pick up in some Turkish bath
His *quantum est* of *Pox Romana*.

While Haakon hikes up primrose way,
Spreeing and gleeing as he goes,
To smirk upon his latter day
Without a pimple on his nose.

I gave it up I am afraid
But if I loafed and found it fun
Remember how a coyclad maid
Knows how to take it out of one.

The more I dither on and drink
My midnight bowl of spirit punch
The firmlier I feel and think
Friend Manders came too oft to lunch.

Since scuttling ship Vikings like me
Reck not to whom the blame is laid,
Y.M.C.A., V.D., T.B.
Or Harbourmaster of Port-Said.

Blame all and none and take to task
The harlot's lure, the swain's desire.
Heal by all means but hardly ask
Did this man sin or did his sire.

The shack's ablaze. That canting scamp,
The carpenter, has dished the parson.
Now had they kept their powder damp
Like me there would have been no arson.

Nay more, were I not all I was,
Weak, wanton, waster out and out,
There would have been no world's applause
And damn all to write home about.

68

Goodbye, Zurich, I must leave you,
Though it breaks my heart to shreds
            Tat then attat.
Something tells me I am needed
In Paree to hump the beds.
Bump! I hear the trunks a tumbling
And I'm frantic for the fray.
Farewell, *dolce far niente*!
Goodbye, Zürichsee!

69

Le bon repos
Des Espagneux
Et les roseaux
  d'Annecy
Leurrent notre âme
Et nous nous pâmons
Pour une Paname
  Loin d'ici

. . . . . .

Tirons nos grègues
Faisons nos mègues
Prenons le trègue
  Et filons là!
Too hot to go on . . .

70

Aiutami dunque, O Musa, nitidissima Calligraphia!
Forbisci la forma e lo stil e frena lo stilo ribelle!
Mesci il limpide suon e distilla il liquido senso
E sulla rena riarsa, deh!, scuoti lungo il ramo!

Come-all-ye

Come all you lairds and ladies and listen to my lay!
I'll tell of my adventures upon last Thanksgiving Day
I was picked by Madame Jolas to adorn the barbecue
So the chickenchoker patched me till I looked as good as
    new.

I drove out, all tarred and feathered, from the Grand Palais
    Potin
But I met with foul disaster in the Place Saint Augustin.
My charioteer collided – with the shock I did explode
And the force of my emotions shot my liver on the road.

Up steps a dapper sergeant with his pencil and his book.
Our names and our convictions down in Leber's code he
    took.
Then I hailed another driver and resumed my swanee way.
They couldn't find my liver but I hadn't time to stay.

When we reached the gates of Paris cries the boss at the
    Octroi:
Holy Poule, what's this I'm seeing? Can it be Grandmother
    Loye?
When Caesar got the bird she was the dindy of the flock
But she must have boxed a round or two with some old
    turkey cock.

I ruffled up my plumage and proclaimed with eagle's pride:
You jackdaw, these are truffles and not blues on my
  backside.
Mind, said he, that one's a chestnut. There's my bill and
  here's my thanks
And now please search through your stuffing and fork out
  that fifty francs.

At last I reached the banquet-hall — and what a sight to see!
I felt myself transported back among the Osmanli.
I poured myself a bubbly flask and raised the golden horn
With three cheers for good old Turkey and the roost where I
  was born.

I shook claws with all the hammers and bowed to blonde
  and brune,
The mistress made a signal and the mujik called the tune.
Madamina read a message from the Big Noise of her State
After which we crowed in unison: That Turco's talking
  straight!

We settled down to feed and, if you want to know my mind,
I thought that I could gobble but they left me picked behind,
They crammed their crops till cockshout when like ostriches
  they ran
To hunt my missing liver round the Place Saint Augustin.

Still I'll lift my glass to Gallia and augur that we may
Untroubled in her dovecot dwell till next Thanksgiving Day
So let every Gallic gander pass the sauceboat to his goose —
And let's all play happy homing though our liver's on the
  loose.

There's a maevusmarked maggot called Murphy
Who would fain be thought thunder-and-turfy.
When he's out to be chic he
Sticks on his gum dicky
And worms off for a breeze by the surfy.

PART II

Shorter Writings

EPIPHANIES

Introduction

Among the writings that survive from Joyce's youth, the earliest important literary compositions are the forty brief prose works he called 'epiphanies' – all that remain of a series that once included at least seventy-one entries. The epiphanies form a bridge between the early poetry and the early fiction, and help us to understand the formative stages of Joyce's art. In the years between 1901–02 and 1904 Joyce recorded crucial fragments of overheard dialogue or personal meditation. He carefully hoarded these fragments, and later – when he had determined their 'spiritual' significance – incorporated many of them into his fictions.

When he first began to collect his epiphanies Joyce regarded them, in the words of his brother Stanislaus, as 'little errors and gestures – mere straws in the wind – by which people betrayed the very things they were most careful to conceal'. The earliest epiphanies were sketches, objective in form and deliberately incomplete; but as Joyce's interest in psychology increased, and his 'theory' of the epiphany became more specific, these dramatic passages were joined by lyrical passages expressing a mood or recounting a dream. Joyce came to think of the epiphanies as moments of artistic radiance, and he advanced this definition in *Stephen Hero*, the early version of *A Portrait of the Artist as a Young Man*:

By an epiphany he [Stephen Dedalus] meant a sudden spiritual manifestation, whether in the vulgarity of speech or of gesture or in a memorable phase of the mind itself. He believed that it was for the man of letters to record these

epiphanies with extreme care, seeing that they themselves
are the most delicate and evanescent of moments.

In this passage Stephen seems to be distinguishing between the
dramatic epiphanies ('the vulgarity of speech or of gesture')
and the lyrical epiphanies that record 'a memorable phase of
the mind itself'. The surviving epiphanies are almost equally
divided between dramatic scenes, often with place indications
and stage directions, and rhythmical prose-poems. The two
kinds of epiphanies represent, therefore, the twin poles of
Joyce's art: dramatic irony and lyric sentiment. At the
moments of highest achievement in Joyce's fiction, the two are
brought together in a manner that enables them to reinforce
each other. Joyce's art is one of both/and, not either/or.
     The best way to understand Joyce's notion of the epiphany
is to see how specific epiphanies were worked into his fictions.
The following scene, one of the most dramatic, became in
revised form the magnificently effective conclusion to the
opening section of *A Portrait of the Artist as a Young Man*:

> [Bray: in the parlour of the house
> in Martello Terrace]
>
> Mr Vance – (*comes in with a stick*) . . . O, you know,
>   he'll have to apologise, Mrs Joyce.
> Mrs Joyce – O yes . . . Do you hear that, Jim?
> Mr Vance – Or else – if he doesn't – the eagles'll
>   come and pull out his eyes.
> Mrs Joyce – O, but I'm sure he will apologise.
> Joyce – (*under the table, to himself*)
>   – Pull out his eyes,
>   Apologise,
>   Apologise,
>   Pull out his eyes.

> Apologise,
> Pull out his eyes,
> Pull out his eyes,
> Apologise.

Even as an isolated incident this epiphany is an arresting account of a sensitive child's confrontation with authority; but the fragment does not become a 'revelation', a radiant image, until it reaches its place in *Portrait* as an introduction to the obsessive themes of guilt and submission. By itself the fragment could only have been radiant to Joyce, since its context is his life. The epiphanies are like an artist's *trouvailles*: their significance lies in the writer's recognition of their potentialities, his faith that a revealing context will eventually be found.

This personal quality of the isolated epiphany is even clearer in lyric passages such as the following, which was ultimately incorporated almost without change into Stephen's diary at the end of *Portrait*.

> The spell of arms and voices – the white arms of roads, their promise of close embraces, and the black arms of tall ships that stand against the moon, their tale of distant nations. They are held out to say: We are alone, – come. And the voices say with them, We are your people. And the air is thick with their company as they call to me their kinsman, making ready to go, shaking the wings of their exultant and terrible youth.

When read in isolation this prose-poem is a haunting but somewhat overwritten adolescent cry, but in the context of *Portrait* it becomes a true manifestation of Stephen's romantic ambitions, sustained and strengthened by the irony that surrounds it.

In *Ulysses* Stephen Dedalus remembers ironically his 'epiphanies on green oval leaves, deeply deep, copies to be sent if you died to all the great libraries of the world, including Alexandria? Someone was to read them there after a few thousand years, a mahamanvantara'. The mature artist who wrote *Ulysses* could afford – indeed was compelled – to look back with mockery on a younger self who had found 'sudden spiritual manifestations' in the drab details of Dublin life. But for us the epiphanies serve a different purpose. They are the purest record we have of the events and feelings that haunted the young James Joyce when he left Dublin in October 1904 to forge in the smithy of his soul the uncreated conscience of his race.

A.W.L.

[Bray: in the parlour of the house
in Martello Terrace]

Mr Vance – (*comes in with a stick*) . . . O, you know,
   he'll have to apologise, Mrs Joyce.
Mrs Joyce – O yes . . . Do you hear that, Jim?
Mr Vance – Or else – if he doesn't – the eagles'll
   come and pull out his eyes.
Mrs Joyce – O, but I'm sure he will apologise.
Joyce – (*under the table, to himself*)
   – Pull out his eyes,
   Apologise,
   Apologise,
   Pull out his eyes.

   Apologise,
   Pull out his eyes,
   Pull out his eyes,
   Apologise.

No school tomorrow: it is Saturday night in winter: I sit by the fire. Soon they will be returning with provisions, meat and vegetables, tea and bread and butter, and white pudding that makes a noise on the pan . . . . I sit reading a story of Alsace, turning over the yellow pages, watching the men and women in their strange dresses. It pleases me to read of their ways; through them I seem to touch the life of a land beyond them to enter into communion with the German people. Dearest illusion, friend of my youth! . . . . In him I have imaged myself. Our lives are still sacred in their intimate sympathies. I am with him at night when he reads the books of the philosophers or some tale of ancient times. I am with him when he wanders alone or with one whom he has never seen, that young girl who puts around him arms that have no malice in them, offering her simple, abundant love, hearing and answering his soul he knows not how.

3

The children who have stayed latest are getting on their things to go home for the party is over. This is the last tram. The lank brown horses know it and shake their bells to the clear night, in admonition. The conductor talks with the driver; both nod often in the green light of the lamp. There is nobody near. We seem to listen, I on the upper step and she on the lower. She comes up to my step many times and goes down again, between our phrases, and once or twice remains beside me, forgetting to go down, and then goes down . . . . . Let be; let be . . . . And now she does not urge her vanities – her fine dress and sash and long black stockings – for now (wisdom of children) we seem to know that this end will please us better than any end we have laboured for.

4

Joyce – (*concludes*) . . . That'll be forty thousand pounds.

Aunt Lillie – (*titters*) – O, laus! . . . . I was like that too. . . . . .
   . . .When I was a girl I was *sure* I'd marry a
   lord . . . or something. . .

Joyce – (*thinks*) – Is it possible she's comparing
   herself with me?

High up in the old, dark-windowed house: firelight in the narrow room: dusk outside. An old woman bustles about, making tea; she tells of the changes, her odd ways, and what the priest and the doctor said . . . . . I hear her words in the distance. I wander among the coals, among the ways of adventure . . . . . . .Christ! What is in the doorway? . . . . .A skull – a monkey; a creature drawn hither to the fire, to the voices: a silly creature.

    – Is that Mary Ellen? –

    – No, Eliza, it's Jim –

    – O. . . . . O, goodnight, Jim –

    – D'ye want anything, Eliza? –

    – I thought it was Mary Ellen . . . . . I thought you were Mary Ellen, Jim –

6

A small field of stiff weeds and thistles alive with confused forms, half-men, half-goats. Dragging their great tails they move hither and thither, aggressively. Their faces are lightly bearded, pointed and grey as india-rubber. A secret personal sin directs them, holding them now, as in reaction, to constant malevolence. One is clasping about his body a torn flannel jacket; another complains monotonously as his beard catches in the stiff weeds. They move about me, enclosing me, that old sin sharpening their eyes to cruelty, swishing through the fields in slow circles, thrusting upwards their terrific faces. Help!

It is time to go away now – breakfast is ready. I'll say another prayer . . . : . I am hungry; yet I would like to stay here in this quiet chapel where the mass has come and gone so quietly . . . . . Hail, holy Queen, Mother of Mercy, our life, our sweetness and our hope! Tomorrow and every day after I hope I shall bring you some virtue as an offering for I know you will be pleased with me if I do. Now, goodbye for the present . . . . . O, the beautiful sunlight in the avenue and O, the sunlight in my heart!

8

Dull clouds have covered the sky. Where three roads meet
and before a swampy beach a big dog is recumbent. From time
to time he lifts his muzzle in the air and utters a prolonged
sorrowful howl. People stop to look at him and pass on; some
remain, arrested, it may be, by that lamentation in which they
seem to hear the utterance of their own sorrow that had once
its voice but is now voiceless, a servant of laborious days. Rain
begins to fall.

9

       [Mullingar: a Sunday in July:
       noon]
Tobin – (walking noisily with thick boots and
    tapping the road with his stick) . . . . O
    there's nothing like marriage for
    making a fellow steady. Before I came
    here to the *Examiner* I used knock about
    with fellows and boose . . . . Now I've a
    good house and . . . . . I go home in the
    evening and if I want a drink . . . . . .
    well, I can have it . . . . My advice to
    every young fellow that can afford it
    is: marry young.

[Dublin: in the Stag's Head,
Dame Lane]

O'Mahony – Haven't you that little priest that
writes poetry over there – Fr Russell?

Joyce – O, yes. . .I hear he has written verses.

O'Mahony – (*smiling adroitly*). . .Verses, yes. . .that's
the proper name for them. . . .

[Dublin: at Sheehy's, Belvedere
Place]

Joyce – I knew you meant him. But you're wrong
about his age.
Maggie Sheehy – (*leans forward to speak seriously*). Why,
how old is he?
Joyce – Seventy-two.
Maggie Sheehy – Is he?

[Dublin: at Sheehy's, Belvedere
Place]

O'Reilly – (*with developing seriousness*). . . .Now
it's my turn, I suppose. . . . .(*quite
seriously*). . . .Who is your favourite
poet?

(*a pause*)

Hanna Sheehy – . . . . . . .German?
O'Reilly – . . . . . .Yes.

(*a hush*)

Hanna Sheehy – . .I think. . . . .Goethe. . . . .

[Dublin: at Sheehy's, Belvedere
Place]

Fallon – (*as he passes*) – I was told to congratulate
    you especially on your performance.

Joyce – Thank you.

Blake – (*after a pause*). .I'd never advise anyone
    to. . .O, it's a terrible life! . . . .

Joyce – Ha.

Blake – (*between puffs of smoke*) – of course. . .it
    looks all right from the outside. . .to
    those who don't know. . . .But if
    you knew. . . .it's really terrible. A
    bit of candle, no. . .dinner, squalid
    . . . .poverty. You've no idea simply. . . .

[Dublin: at Sheehy's, Belvedere
Place]

Dick Sheehy – What's a lie? Mr Speaker, I must ask. . .

Mr Sheehy – Order, order!

Fallon – You know it's a lie!

Mr Sheehy – You must withdraw, sir.

Dick Sheehy – As I was saying. . . .

Fallon – No, I won't.

Mr Sheehy – I call on the honourable member
for Denbigh. . . . Order, order! . . .

[In Mullingar: an evening
in autumn]

The Lame Beggar – (*gripping his stick*). . . .It was
you called out after me yesterday.

The Two Children – (*gazing at him*). . .No, sir.

The Lame Beggar – O, yes it was, though. . . .(*moving
his stick up and down*). . . .But
mind what I'm telling you. . . .
D'ye see that stick?

The Two Children – Yes, sir.

The Lame Beggar – Well, if ye call out after me
any more I'll cut ye open with
that stick. I'll cut the livers
out o'ye. . . .(*explains himself*)
. . . D'ye hear me? I'll cut ye
open. I'll cut the livers and
the lights out o'ye.

A white mist is falling in slow flakes. The path leads me down to an obscure pool. Something is moving in the pool; it is an arctic beast with a rough yellow coat. I thrust in my stick and as he rises out of the water I see that his back slopes towards the croup and that he is very sluggish. I am not afraid but, ·thrusting at him often with my stick drive him before me. He moves his paws heavily and mutters words of some language which I do not understand.

[Dublin: at Sheehy's, Belvedere
Place]

Hanna Sheehy – O, there are sure to be great crowds.

Skeffington – In fact it'll be, as our friend
Jocax would say, the day of the
rabblement.

Maggie Sheehy – (*declaims*) – Even now the
rabblement may be standing
by the door!

[Dublin, on the North Circular
Road: Christmas]

Miss O'Callaghan — (*lisps*) — I told you the name,
The Escaped Nun.

Dick Sheehy — (*loudly*) — O, I wouldn't read
a book like that. . .I must
ask Joyce. I say, Joyce, did
you ever read *The Escaped
Nun?*

Joyce — I observe that a certain
phenomenon happens about
this hour.

Dick Sheehy — What phenomenon?

Joyce — O. . .the stars come out.

Dick Sheehy — (*to Miss O'Callaghan*). .Did you
ever observe how. . .the
stars come out on the end
of Joyce's nose about this
hour? . . .(*she smiles*). .Because
I observe that phenomenon.

[Dublin: in the house in
Glengariff Parade: evening]

Mrs Joyce – (*crimson, trembling, appears at the
parlour door*). . .Jim!

Joyce – (*at the piano*). . .Yes?

Mrs Joyce – Do you know anything about the
body? . . .What ought I do?. . .There's
some matter coming away from
the hole in Georgie's stomach. . . .
Did you ever hear of that happening?

Joyce – (*surprised*). . .I don't know. . . .

Mrs Joyce – Ought I send for the doctor, do you
think?

Joyce – I don't know. . . . . .What hole?

Mrs Joyce – (*impatient*). . .The hole we all have
. . . . .here (*points*)

Joyce – (*stands up*)

They are all asleep. I will go up now . . . . . He lies on my bed where I lay last night: they have covered him with a sheet and closed his eyes with pennies. . . . Poor little fellow! We have often laughed together — he bore his body very lightly . . . . I am very sorry he died. I cannot pray for him as the others do . . . . . Poor little fellow! Everything else is so uncertain!

Two mourners push on through the crowd. The girl, one hand catching the woman's skirt, runs in advance. The girl's face is the face of a fish, discoloured and oblique-eyed; the woman's face is small and square, the face of a bargainer. The girl, her mouth distorted, looks up at the woman to see if it is time to cry; the woman, settling a flat bonnet, hurries on towards the mortuary chapel.

[Dublin: in the National Library]

Skeffington – I was sorry to hear of the death of
your brother. . . .sorry we didn't
know in time. . . . .to have been at
the funeral. . . . .

Joyce – O, he was very young. . . .a boy. . . .

Skeffington – Still. . . . .it hurts. . . .

That is no dancing. Go down before the people, young boy, and dance for them. . . . He runs out darkly-clad, lithe and serious to dance before the multitude. There is no music for him. He begins to dance far below in the amphitheatre with a slow and supple movement of the limbs, passing from move-ment to movement, in all the grace of youth and distance, until he seems to be a whirling body, a spider wheeling amid space, a star. I desire to shout to him words of praise, to shout arrogantly over the heads of the multitude 'See! See!' . . . . . His dancing is not the dancing of harlots, the dance of the daughters of Herodias. It goes up from the midst of the people, sudden and young and male, and falls again to earth in tremulous sobbing to die upon its triumph.

Her arm is laid for a moment on my knees and then withdrawn, and her eyes have revealed her — secret, vigilant, an enclosed garden — in a moment. I remember a harmony of red and white that was made for one like her, telling her names and glories, bidding her arise as for espousal, and come away, bidding her look forth, a spouse, from Amana and from the mountain of the leopards. And I remember that response whereunto the perfect tenderness of the body and the soul with all its mystery have gone: Inter ubera mea commorabitur.

25

The quick light shower is over but tarries, a cluster of diamonds, among the shrubs of the quadrangle where an exhalation arises from the black earth. In the colonnade are the girls, an April company. They are leaving shelter, with many a doubting glance, with the prattle of trim boots and the pretty rescue of petticoats, under umbrellas, a light armoury, upheld at cunning angles. They are returning to the convent – demure corridors and simple dormitories, a white rosary of hours – having heard the fair promises of Spring, that well-graced ambassador . . . .

Amid a flat rain-swept country stands a high plain building, with windows that filter the obscure daylight. Three hundred boys, noisy and hungry, sit at long tables eating beef fringed with green fat and vegetables that are still rank of the earth.

She is engaged. She dances with them in the round – a white dress lightly lifted as she dances, a white spray in her hair; eyes a little averted, a faint glow on her cheek. Her hand is in mine for a moment, softest of merchandise.

– You very seldom come here now. –

– Yes I am becoming something of a recluse. –

– I saw your brother the other day . . . . . . He is
   very like you. –

– Really? –

She dances with them in the round – evenly, discreetly, giving herself to no one. The white spray is ruffled as she dances, and when she is in shadow the glow is deeper on her cheek.

Faintly, under the heavy summer night, through the silence
of the town which has turned from dreams to dreamless sleep
as a weary lover whom no caresses move, the sound of hoofs
upon the Dublin road. Not so faintly now as they come near
the bridge; and in a moment as they pass the dark windows the
silence is cloven by alarm as by an arrow. They are heard now
far away – hoofs that shine amid the heavy night as diamonds,
hurrying beyond the grey, still marshes to what journey's end –
what heart – bearing what tidings?

A moonless night under which the waves gleam feebly. The ship is entering a harbour where there are some lights. The sea is uneasy, charged with dull anger like the eyes of an animal which is about to spring, the prey of its own pitiless hunger. The land is flat and thinly wooded. Many people are gathered on the shore to see what ship it is that is entering their harbour.

A long curving gallery: from the floor arise pillars of dark vapours. It is peopled by the images of fabulous kings, set in stone. Their hands are folded upon their knees, in token of weariness, and their eyes are darkened for the errors of men go up before them for ever as dark vapours.

The spell of arms and voices — the white arms of roads, their promise of close embraces, and the black arms of tall ships that stand against the moon, their tale of distant nations. They are held out to say: We are alone, — come. And the voices say with them, We are your people. And the air is thick with their company as they call to me their kinsman, making ready to go, shaking the wings of their exultant and terrible youth.

Here are we come together, wayfarers; here are we housed, amid intricate streets, by night and silence closely covered. In amity we rest together, well content, no more remembering the deviousness of the ways that we have come. What moves upon me from the darkness subtle and murmurous as a flood, passionate and fierce with an indecent movement of the loins? What leaps, crying in answer, out of me, as eagle to eagle in mid air, crying to overcome, crying for an iniquitous abandonment?

The human crowd swarms in the enclosure, moving through the slush. A fat woman passes, her dress lifted boldly, her face nozzling in an orange. A pale young man with a Cockney accent does tricks in his shirtsleeves and drinks out of a bottle. A little old man has mice on an umbrella; a policeman in heavy boots charges down and seizes the umbrella: the little old man disappears. Bookies are bawling out names and prices; one of them screams with the voice of a child – 'Bonny Boy!' 'Bonny Boy!' . . . Human creatures are swarming in the enclosure, moving backwards and forwards through the thick ooze. Some ask if the race is going on; they are answered 'Yes' and 'No.' A band begins to play. . . . . . A beautiful brown horse, with a yellow rider upon him, flashes far away in the sunlight.

33

They pass in twos and threes amid the life of the boulevard, walking like people who have leisure in a place lit up for them. They are in the pastry cook's, chattering, crushing little fabrics of pastry, or seated silently at tables by the café door, or descending from carriages with a busy stir of garments soft as the voice of the adulterer. They pass in an air of perfumes: under the perfumes their bodies have a warm humid smell . . . . . No man has loved them and they have not loved themselves: they have given nothing for all that has been given them.

34

She comes at night when the city is still; invisible, inaudible, all unsummoned. She comes from her ancient seat to visit the least of her children, mother most venerable, as though he had never been alien to her. She knows the inmost heart; therefore she is gentle, nothing exacting; saying, I am susceptible of change, an imaginative influence in the hearts of my children. Who has pity for you when you are sad among the strangers? Years and years I loved you when you lay in my womb.

35

[London: in a house at
Kennington]

Eva Leslie – Yes, Maudie Leslie's my sister an'
     Fred Leslie's my brother – yev
     'eard of Fred Leslie? . . . (*musing*) . . .
     O,'e's a whoite-arsed bugger. . .'E's
     awoy at present. . . . . . .
              (*later*)
     I told you someun went with me
     ten toimes one noight. . . .That's
     Fred – my own brother Fred. . . .
     (*musing*). . .'E is 'andsome . . .O I
     do love Fred. . . .

Yes, they are the two sisters. She who is churning with stout arms (their butter is famous) looks dark and unhappy: the other is happy because she had her way. Her name is R. . . . Rina. I know the verb 'to be' in their language.

     – Are you Rina? –

I knew she was.

But here he is himself in a coat with tails and an old-fashioned high hat. He ignores them: he walks along with tiny steps, jutting out the tails of his coat. . . . My goodness! how small he is! He must be very old and vain. . . . .Maybe he isn't what I. . .It's funny that those two big women fell out over this little man. . . .But then he's the greatest man in the world. . . .

I lie along the deck, against the engine-house, from which the smell of lukewarm grease exhales. Gigantic mists are marching under the French cliffs, enveloping the coast from headland to headland. The sea moves with the sound of many scales. . . . Beyond the misty walls, in the dark cathedral church of Our Lady, I hear the bright, even voices of boys singing before the altar there.

38

                    [Dublin: at the corner of
                    Connaught St, Phibsborough]

The Little Male Child – (*at the garden gate*). .Na. .o.
The First Young Lady – (*half kneeling, takes his
        hand*) – Well, is Mabie
    your sweetheart?
The Little Male Child – Na. . .o.
The Second Young Lady – (*bending over him, looks
        up*) – *Who* is your
    sweetheart?

39

She stands, her book held lightly at her breast, reading the lesson. Against the dark stuff of her dress her face, mild-featured with downcast eyes, rises softly outlined in light; and from a folded cap, set carelessly forward, a tassel falls along her brown ringletted hair . . .

What is the lesson that she reads — of apes, of strange inventions, or the legends of martyrs? Who knows how deeply meditative, how reminiscent is this comeliness of Raffaello?

in O'Connell St:
[Dublin: ∧ in Hamilton, Long's,
the chemist's,]

Gogarty – Is that for Gogarty?

pay

The Assistant – (*looks*) – Yes, sir. . .Will you ~~take
it with you?~~ for it now?

Gogarty – No, ~~send it~~ put it in the
account; send it on. You know
the address.

(*takes a pen*)

The Assistant – ~~Yes~~   Ye–es.

Gogarty – 5 Rutland Square.

while

The Assistant – (*half to himself ~~as~~ he writes*)
. . 5. . .*Rutland*. . .Square.

A PORTRAIT OF THE ARTIST

1904

Introduction

On 7 January 1904 James Joyce copied an essay entitled 'A Portrait of the Artist' into an exercise book belonging to his sister Mabel. In the same month he submitted it to W. K. Magee, editor and co-founder of a new periodical, *Dana, a magazine of independent thought*. Magee declined to publish Joyce's 'Portrait', but this rejection, as Stanislaus Joyce reported in his diary (2 February 1904), proved fortunate:

Jim . . . has decided to turn his paper into a novel, and having come to that decision is just as glad, he says, that it was rejected. . . . Jim is beginning his novel, as he usually begins things, half in anger, to show that in writing about himself he has a subject of more interest than their aimless discussion.

Far from being aimless himself, Joyce had written the initial chapter of *Stephen Hero* within a month and worked diligently at his first novel over the next three years before recasting his narrative as *A Portrait of the Artist as a Young Man*.

Looking back at Joyce's autobiographical essay, readers of 'A Portrait of the Artist' have smiled at Magee's response: 'I handed it back to him with the timid observation that I did not care to publish what was to myself incomprehensible. . . . I imagine that what he showed me was some early attempt in fiction.' However, Magee's bewildered evaluation is worth recalling because it addresses the essay's fundamental peculiarity. Joyce's brief self-portrait is an extraordinarily dense piece of writing, a fact we are likely to overlook if we treat the essay as an abandoned quarry or an early snapshot – searching only for fragments that turn up in *Stephen Hero* and *Portrait*, uncovering isolate features that are perfectly defined in the mature Joyce. The difficulties of Joyce's later work are present here on a reduced scale: the syntax and texture of allusion tangled, the tone various and difficult to ascertain, the narrator's approach changing within a single paragraph. Instead of reading 'A Portrait of the Artist' simply as a preface to *Portrait*, we should follow the essay along its own curious path.

The pursuit of Joyce's sense is not easy. Virtually every sentence in the first two paragraphs resists interpretation. Individual words and phrases remain puzzling no matter how often we reread them: Why are we 'capricious' in our conception of the past? What, precisely, does it mean that the 'world . . . recognises its acquaintance'? Circumlocutions render the familiar strange: signs of ageing become 'characters of beard and inches'; 'to liberate from the personalised lumps of matter that which is their individuating rhythm' is to make a self-portrait. And even that portrait is not what we would think, not 'an identificative paper', but 'the curve of an emotion'. The phrase hints at a concrete visual figure in 'curve' but leaves us with the intangible 'emotion'. Nor will the portrait begin, as the first sentence had suggested, with 'the features of infancy'. The second paragraph informs us that we will commence after the boy has achieved 'use of reason', which is 'antedated [by] some seven years'. The first specific glimpse of the subject comes indirectly, through the eyes of 'a labourer', who sees 'a boy of fifteen praying in an ecstasy of Oriental posture' (that labourer, were he to tell the story, would say the boy was 'facing east').

If Joyce had continued 'A Portrait of the Artist' in the same prolix vein we might easily dismiss the essay for its annoying obscurity. But in the third paragraph he offers both dramatic stylistic shifts and an explanation for the preceding mystification. Upon his entrance to the University, 'the enigma of a manner was put up at all comers to protect the crisis'. That 'crisis' is the search for the self's 'individuating rhythm' with which the 'Portrait' opens. In order to 'disentangle his affairs in secrecy', the artist quickly learns how to hide behind ostensible self-disclosure. Stanislaus, whose diary records his brother's protective poses, is the first critic to comment upon James's cultivation of masks:

Jim is thought to be very frank about himself, but his style is such that it might be contended that he confesses in a foreign language – an easier confession than in the vulgar tongue.

It is in the third paragraph of 'Portrait' that Joyce demonstrates his fluency in several stylistic languages. In an appropriately extended epic simile he unveils a cherished heroic emblem of himself as a deer pursued by hounds. He follows the simile with a 'diagnosis' of his classmates that is 'exquisite, deliberate, sharp' – its sudden lucidity remarkable. The scene shifts again when student becomes 'alchemist' among the 'hierarchs of initiation'. His ringing cadences proclaim apocalypse even as vague passive verbs reveal the hopelessness of his aims: 'A thousand eternities were to be reaffirmed, divine knowledge was to be re-established.' Quickly recovering from his own deluded idealism, the young spiritualist sneers at the 'blue triangles' and 'fish-gods' dear to theosophy and the Irish folk revival. The alchemist who had subtly combined 'the mysterious elements' now practises a less refined chemistry: 'He lumped the emancipates together . . .'

The set-piece of Joyce's essay, and the point at which we are allowed the most sustained, revealing view of the developing artist, is the seaside episode. It contains the seeds of two opposed scenes in *Portrait*: Stephen's surrender to the prostitute at the end of the second chapter, and his vision of the 'angel of mortal youth' at the end of the fourth. Although this first version lacks the emotional weight of the later scenes, it perfectly displays Joyce's technique of allowing his characters to cast their stories in their own revealing terms. The adolescent in the essay claims grandiloquently to desire 'isolation'. His partially willed ignorance of his essentially sexual goals gives the narrative comic tension. The lyrical phrases that describe his evening wanderings recur whenever Joyce evokes 'meditative hours' in his writings. The prose exhibits the 'romantic temper' characterized in *Stephen Hero* as 'an insecure, unsatisfied, impatient temper which sees no fit abode here for its ideals and chooses therefore to behold them under insensible figures'. Already Joyce knows how to qualify this dreamy self-indulgence by introducing concrete detail into an insubstantial, imaginary setting. The romance of the boy's journey is undercut when we learn, in a parenthetical admission, that he is 'avowedly in quest of shellfish'.

At this moment in Joyce's narrative of the adolescent's seaside rambles, readers conditioned by *A Portrait of the Artist as a Young Man* expect to be shown, instead of shellfish, a modest, birdlike girl gazing out to sea. She is nowhere on the strand in 'Portrait': there is no fitting object to engage the young man's longing. He recalls a ponderous quotation from St Augustine; the words do nothing to calm his ardour. He turns quickly to his boyhood memory of sexual initiation with a prostitute, but he summons that memory in absurdly overwrought phrases. The grotesque mismatching of style and event transforms the meeting with the 'beneficent one' into burlesque. The adolescent, much like the boy in 'Araby', describes his 'enrichment of soul', his narrative all the while suffused with body. A distinction Joyce makes in *Stephen Hero* is apposite. The romantic's desires are 'lacking the gravity of solid bodies', while 'the classical temper . . . chooses rather to bend upon . . . present things . . .'

'Present things' show through each ethereal sentence after the first embrace: 'Thy disposition could refine and direct his passion, holding mere beauty at the cunningest angle.' Almost every word in this seemingly abstract sentence doubles as comic evasion and as ribald pun. Joyce praises the woman's 'disposition' (the placement of her body as well as her temperament) that allows her to 'refine and direct' his passion. Both verbs and the noun 'passion' have specific physical connotations, as does the woman's ability to hold 'mere beauty' at an 'angle' for her partner; the adjective 'cunningest' scarcely conceals the anatomical reference. In the following phrase – 'very visible grace' – the adverb, adjective, and context all shift the noun from its theological centre. The pace is momentarily broken by a reminiscence whose disjunctive style exemplifies the scene's broader narrative design: 'In another phase it had been not uncommon to devise dinners in white and purple upon the actuality of stirabout.' This pompous digression then tumbles into bawdy exhortation: 'but here, surely, is sturdy or delicate food to hand; no need for devising.'

Self-encouragement and circuitous directions to 'the measurable world and the broad expanses of activity' precede the climax of this meeting. These nervous strategies have their psychological reflections in *Portrait*, when Stephen first retreats from the prostitute and then avoids thought in her arms:

– Give me a kiss, she said.
His lips would not bend to kiss her. . . . He closed his eyes, surrendering himself to her, body and mind, conscious of

nothing in the world but the dark pressure of her softly parting lips.

Joyce achieves sustained effects in his novel by separating the scene of Stephen's sexual initiation from his hero's quasi-religious encounter with the feminine embodiment of 'mortal youth and beauty' on the strand. And yet this early conflation of material creates an exemplary occasion for the vivid, emotionally suggestive comedy that illuminates all of Joyce's subsequent work.

The multivalent comedy continues in the last paragraph of Joyce's 'Portrait', which shows the young artist venturing out into the world. His conduct in public is a hodgepodge of inappropriate, contradictory gestures that are syntactically yoked together without revealing any clear 'formal relation' to each other: 'He had interpreted for orthodox Greek scholarship the living doctrine of the *Poetics* and, out of the burning bushes of excess, had declaimed to a night-policeman on the true status of public women.' Stephen Dedalus similarly lacks a sense of audience, as his analogous declamations to Private Carr in 'Circe' demonstrate. The irresistible urge towards prophecy, towards effecting change through words, drives the artist to increasingly global proclamations. The heated peroration that closes 'A Portrait of the Artist' refers in passing to political events and deploys socialist rhetoric, but it is modelled on divine rather than secular intervention: 'To those multitudes, not as yet in the wombs of humanity but surely engenderable there, he would give the word.'

It is important to recall the prelude to this gigantic hope. Just before the conclusion of 'Portrait', Joyce's young hero has delivered a violent 'outburst' against the church and has then vowed to practise 'urbanity in warfare'. His instantaneous failure to conduct his campaign diplomatically helps to explain why Joyce's 'Portrait' baffles: it is difficult to create a coherent portrait of the artist when the subject can only temporarily compose himself inside a frame. The essay closes with a millenarian vision of international political awakening, but this hope for global unity recalls the more intimate opening of Joyce's essay. The final dream of a truly 'confederate will' emerging from social paralysis suggests a perfected psychological state – a will in league with itself, a united internal assembly.

At the beginning of this 'Portrait' we are told confidently that the self is made up of 'features', developed from infancy to adulthood, that may be drawn in a single 'curve'. Joyce proposes that a portrait, more ambitious than a simple 'identificative paper', will reveal the 'rhythm' uniquely characteristic of its subject. The disquieting variety of 'parts' within a self will be shown to have a 'first or formal relation' among themselves. 'A Portrait of the Artist' has challenged these assertions. The riddles of portraiture grow more profoundly mystifying in Joyce's succeeding works, but they are posed in his first sketch.

J. W.-F.

A Portrait of the Artist[1]

The features of infancy are not commonly reproduced in the adolescent portrait for, so capricious are we, that we cannot or will not conceive the past in any other than its iron memorial aspect. Yet the past assuredly implies a fluid succession of presents, the development of an entity of which our actual present is a phase only.[2] Our world, again, recognises its acquaintance chiefly by the characters of beard and inches and is, for the most part, estranged from those of its members who seek through some art, by some process of the mind as yet untabulated, to liberate from the personalised lumps of matter that which is their individuating rhythm, the first or formal relation of their parts.[3] But for such as these a portrait is not an identificative paper but rather the curve of an emotion.

Use of reason is by popular judgment antedated [by] some seven years and so it is not easy to set down the exact age at which the natural [s]ens[ibi]lity of the subject of this portrait awok[e to the ide]as of eternal damnation, the necessi[ty of peni]tence and the efficacy of prayer. <H[is t]raining had early developed a very lively sense of spiritual obligations at the expense of [wh]at is called 'common sense'. He ran through his measure like a spendthrift s[aint], astonishing many by ejaculatory f[erv]ours, offending many by airs of the cloister. One day in a wood near Malahide a labourer had marvelled to see a boy of fifteen praying in an ecstasy of Oriental posture.[4] It was indeed a long time before this boy understood the nature of that most marketable goodness which makes it possible to give comfortable assent to propositions without ordering one's life in accordance with them.[5] The digestive value of religion he

never appreciated[6] and he chose, as more fitting his case, those poorer, humbler orders in which a confessor did not seem anxious to reveal himself, in theory at least, a man of the world.[7] In spite, however, of continued shocks, which drove him from breathless flights of zeal shamefully inwards, he was still soothed by devotional exercises when he entered the University.

About this period the enigma of a manner was put up at all comers to protect the crisis.[8] He was quick enough now to see that he must disentangle his affairs in secrecy and reserve had ever been a light penance. His reluctance to debate scandal, to seem curious of others, aided him in his real indictment and was not without a satisfactory flavour of the heroic.[9] It was part of that ineradicable egoism which he was afterwards to call redeemer that he imagined converging to him the deeds and thoughts of the microcosm.[10] Is the mind of boyhood medieval that it is so divining of intrigue? Field sports (or their correspondents in the world of mentality) are perhaps the most effective cure, but for this fantastic idealist, eluding the grunting booted apparition with a bound, the mimic hunt was no less ludicrous than unequal in a ground chosen to his disadvantage.[11] But behind the rapidly indurating shield the sensitive answered. Let the pack of enmities come tumbling and sniffing to the highlands after their game; there was his ground; and he flung them disdain from flashing antlers.>[12] There was evident self-flattery in the image but a danger of complacence too. Wherefore, neglecting the wheezier bayings in tha[t Cho]rus which no leagues of distance could make musical,[13] he began loftily diagnosis of the younglings. His judgment was exquisite, deliberate, sharp; his sentence sculptural. <These young men saw in the sudden death of a dull French novelist[14] the hand of Emmanuel – God with us; they admired Gla[d]stone,[15] physical science and the tragedies of

Shakespeare; and they believed in the adjustment of Catholic teaching to everyday needs, in the Church diplomatic.[16] In their relations among themselves and towards their superiors they displayed a nervous and (wherever there was question of authority) a very English liberalism>. He remarked the half-admiring, half-reproving demeanour of a class, implicitly pledged to abstinences towards <others among whom (the fame went) wild living was not unknown.[17] Though the union of faith and fatherland was ever sacred in that world of easily inflammable enthusiasms a couplet from Davis,[18] accusing the least docile of tempers, – never failed of its applause and the memory of McManus[19] was hardly less revered than that of Cardinal Cullen>.[20] They had many reasons to respect authority; and even if <a student were forbidden to go to *Othello* ("There are some coarse expressions in it" he was told.) what a little cross was that?[21] Was it not rather an evidence of watchful care and interest, and were they not assured that in their future lives this care would continue, this interest be maintained? The exercise of authority might be sometimes (rarely) questionable, its intention, never. Who, therefore, readier than these young men to acknowledge gratefully the sallies of some genial professor or the surliness of some door-porter, who more sollicitous to cherish in every way and to advance in person the honour of Alma Mater? For his part he was at the difficult age, dispossessed and necessitous,[22] sensible of all that was ignoble in such manners who, in revery at least, had been acquainted with nobility.[23] An earnest Jesuit had prescribed a clerkship in Guinness's:[24] and doubtless the clerk-designate of a brewery would not have had scorn and pity only for an admirable community had it not been that he desired (in the language of the schoolmen) an arduous good.[25] It was possible that he should find solace in [so]cieties for the encouragement of thought among laymen or any other than

bodily comfort in the warm sodality[26] amid so many foolish or grotesque virginities.[27] Moreover, it was impossible that a temperament ever trembling towards its ecstasy should submit to acquiesce, that a soul should decree servitude for its portion over which the image of beauty had fallen as a mantle.[28] One night in early spring, standing at the foot of the staircase in the library, he said to his friend "I have left the Church."> And as they walked home through the streets arm-in-arm he told, in words that seemed an echo of their closing, how he had left it through the gates of Assisi.[29]

Extravagance followed:[30] The simple history of the Poverello[31] was soon out of mind and he established himself in the maddest of companies. Joachim Abbas,[32] Bruno the Nolan,[33] Michael Sendivogius,[34] all the hierarchs of initiation cast their spells upon him. He descended among the hells of Swedenborg[35] and abased himself in the gloom of Saint John of the Cross.[36] His heaven was suddenly illumined by a horde of stars, the signatures of all nature, the soul remembering ancient days.[37] Like an alchemist he bent upon his handiwork, bringing together the mysterious elements, separating the subtle from the gross.[38] For the artist the rhythms of phrase and period, the symbols of word and allusion, were paramount things.[39] And was it any wonder that out of this marvellous life, wherein he had annihilated and rebuilt experience, laboured and despaired, he came forth at last with a single purpose – to reunite the children of the spirit, jealous and long-divided, to reunite them against fraud and principality. A thousand eternities were to be reaffirmed, divine knowledge was to be re-established. Alas for Fatuity! as easily might he have summoned a regiment of the winds. They pleaded their natural pieties – social limitations, inherited apathy of race, an adoring mother, the Christian fable.[40] Their treasons were venial only. Wherever the social monster permitted they would hazard the extremes of heterodoxy; reasons of an imaginative determinant in ethics, of anarchy (the folk), of blue triangles,[41] [o]f the fish-gods,[42] proclaiming in a fervent moment the necessity for action. His revenge was a phrase and isolation. He lumped the emancipates together – Venomous Butter – and set away from the sloppy neighbour-hood.[43]

Isolation, he had once written, is the first principle of artistic economy[44] but traditional and individual revelations were at that time pressing their claims and self-communion had been but shyly welcomed. But in the intervals of friendships (for he [had] outridden three) he had known the sisterhood of meditative hours and now the hope began to grow up within him of finding among them that serene emotion, that certitude, which among men he had not found. An impulse had led him forth in the dark season to silent and lonely places where the mists hung streamerwise among the trees; and as he had passed there amid the subduing night, in the secret fall of leaves, the fragrant rain, the mesh of vapours moon-trans-pierced, he had imagined an admonition of the frailty of all things/.[45] In summer it had led him seaward[.][46] Wandering over the arid, grassy hills or along the strand, avowedly in quest of shellfish, he had grown almost impatient of the day. Waders, into whose childish or girlish hair, girlish or childish dresses, the very wilfulness of the sea had entered – even they had not fascinated.[47] But as day had waned it had been pleasant to watch the few last figures islanded in distant pools; and as evening deepened the grey glow above the sea he had gone out, out among the shallow waters, the holy joys of solitude uplifting him, singing passionately to the tide/[.][48] Sceptically, cynically, mystically, he had sought for an absolute satisfaction and now little by little he began to be conscious of the beauty of mortal conditions. He remembered a sentence in Augustine – "It was manifested unto me that those things be good which yet are corrupted; which neither if they are supremely good, nor unless they were good could be corrupted: for had they been [su]premely good they would have been [in]corruptible but if they were not good [the]re would be nothing in them which could [be c]orrupted".[49] A philosophy of reconcilement [possible . . .] as eve[. . . .] Th[. . .] of the [. . .] at lef[. . .] bor [. . .][50] lit up with dolphin lights,[51] but the lights in the chambers of the heart were unextinguished, nay, burning as for espousal.

Dearest of mortals! In spite of tributary verses and of the comedy of meetings here and in the foolish society of sleep the fountain of being (it seemed) had been interfused.[52] Years before, in boyhood, <the energy of sin opening a world before him> he had been made aware of thee.[53] <The yellow gaslamps arising in his troubled vision, against an autumnal sky, gleaming mysteriously there before that violet altar – the groups gathered at the doorways arrayed as for some rite – the glimpses of revel and fantasmal mirth – [54] the vague face of some welcomer seeming to awaken from a slumber of centuries under his gaze[55] – the blind confusion (iniquity! iniquity!) suddenly overtaking him – in all that ardent adventure of lust didst thou not even then communicate>? Beneficent one! (the shrewdness of love was in the title) thou camest timely, as a witch to the agony of the self-devourer, an envoy from the fair courts of life.[56] How could he thank thee for that enrichment of soul by thee consummated? Mastery of art had been achieved in irony; asceticism of intellect had been a mood of indignant pride: but who had revealed him to himself but thou alone? In ways of tenderness, simple, intuitive tenderness, thy love had made to arise in him the central torrents of life. Thou hadst put thine arms about him and, intimately prisoned as thou hadst been, in the soft stir of thy bosom, the raptures of silence, the murmured words, thy heart had spoken to his heart. Thy disposition could refine and direct his passion, holding mere beauty at the cunningest angle.[57] Thou wert sacramental, imprinting thine indelible mark, of very visible grace. A litany must honour thee;[58] Lady of the Apple Trees,[59] Kind Wisdom, Sweet Flower of Dusk. In another phase it had been not uncommon to devise dinners in white and purple upon the actuality of stirabout[60] but here, surely, is sturdy or delicate food to hand; no need for devising. His way (abrupt creature!) lies out now to the measurable world and [t]he broad expanses of activity. The blood hurries to a galop in his veins; his nerves accumulate an electric force; he is footed with flame. A kiss: and they leap together, indivisible, upwards, radiant lips and eyes, their bodies sounding with the triumph of harps! Again, beloved! Again, thou bride! Again, ere life is ours!

In calmer mood the critic in him could not but remark a strange prelude to the new crowning era in a season of melancholy and unrest. He made up his tale of losses − a dispiriting tale enough even were there no comments.[61] The air of false Christ was manifestly the mask of a physical decrepitude, itself the brand and sign of vulgar ardours;[62] whence ingenuousness, forbearance, sweet amiability and the whole tribe of domestic virtues. Sadly mindful of the worst the vision of his dead, the vision (far more pitiful) of congenital lives shuffling onwards between yawn and howl,[63] starvelings in mind and body, visions of which came a temporary failure of his olden, sustained manner, darkly beset him. The cloud of difficulties about him allowed only peeps of light; even his rhetoric proclaimed transition. He could convict himself at least of a natural inability to prove everything at once and certain random attempts suggested the need for regular campaigning.[64] His faith increased. It emboldened him to say to a patron of the fine arts[65] 'What advance upon spiritual goods?' and to a capitalist[66] 'I need two thousand pounds for a project'. He had interpreted for orthodox Greek scholarship the living doctrine of the *Poetics*[67] and, out of the burning bushes of excess, had declaimed to a night-policeman on the true status of public women:[68] but there was no budge of those mountains, no perilous cerebration. In a moment of frenzy he called for the elves.[69] Many[70] in our day, it would appear, cannot avoid a choice between sensitiveness and dulness; they recommend themselves by proofs of culture[71] to a like-minded minority or dominate the huger world as lean of meat. But he saw between camps his ground of vantage, opportunities for the mocking devil[72] in an isle twice removed from the mainland, under joint government of Their Intensities and Their Bullockships.[73] His Nego,[74] therefore, written amid a chorus of peddling Jews' gibberish and Gentile clamour, was drawn up valiantly while true believers prophesied fried atheism and was hurled against the obscene hells of our Holy Mother:[75] but, that outburst over, it was urbanity in warfare. Perhaps his state would pension off old tyranny – a mercy no longer hopelessly remote – in virtue of that mature civilisation to which (let all allow) it had in some way contributed.[76] Already the messages of citizens were flashed along the wires of the world, already the generous idea had emerged from a thirty years' war in Germany[77] and was directing the councils of the Latins.[78] To those multitudes, not as yet in the wombs of humanity but surely engenderable there, he would give the word:[79] Man and woman, out of you comes the nation that is to come, the lightning[80] of your masses in travail; the competitive order is employed against itself,[81] the aristocracies are supplanted; and amid the general paralysis of an insane society,[82] the confederate will issues in action.

Jas. A. Joyce
7/1/1904/.

[218]

GIACOMO JOYCE

Introduction

James Joyce wrote *Giacomo Joyce* over half a century ago in Trieste, at that stage of his life when he was completing *A Portrait of the Artist as a Young Man* and was beginning *Ulysses*. *Giacomo Joyce* pivots between the two books. A love poem which is never recited, it is Joyce's farewell to a phase of life, and his discovery of a new form of imaginative expression.

Joyce abandoned the manuscript of *Giacomo Joyce* in Trieste when he left the city for Zurich in 1915 because of the war. It was saved from loss by his brother Stanislaus. Joyce wrote the work in his best calligraphic hand, without changes, on both sides of eight large sheets, which are loosely held within the nondescript grey-paper covers of a school notebook. The sheets are of heavy paper, oversize, of the sort ordinarily used for pencil sketches rather than for writing assignments. They are faintly reminiscent of those parchment sheets on which in 1909 Joyce wrote out the poems of *Chamber Music* for his wife. On the upper left-hand corner of the front cover, the name 'Giacomo Joyce' is inscribed in another hand. Joyce was content to keep what he had written under this heading, the Italian form of his name, and it has seemed reasonable to follow his example. Joyce allows no doubt that the hero is to be identified with himself; Giacomo calls himself 'Jamesy' and 'Jim', and once appeals to his wife as 'Nora'.

Giacomo Joyce displays its hero's erotic commotion over a girl pupil to whom he was teaching English. Joyce had many such pupils in Trieste, but he seems to associate his subject with one in particular, Amalia Popper, who lived on the via

Alice, off the via San Michele. According to her later recollections (and those of her husband), her tutelage by Joyce lasted from as early as 1907 to as late as 1911. Signorina Popper became engaged to Michele Risolo during the Easter holidays of 1913 and married him in August 1914. Her father, Leopoldo Popper, may have furnished the first name for Bloom in *Ulysses*. But if he stood as a model for the pupil's father in *Giacomo Joyce*, he was made to give up his imposing moustache and take on unaccustomed whiskers. Ultimately, both father and daughter in Joyce's text are biographically composite figures. The work makes clear, at any rate, that the incident – such as it was – ended before he left Trieste in 1915.

Joyce's prose writings are so committed to an Irish scene that among them *Giacomo Joyce* is distinct in being set on the Continent. The city of Trieste, like Dublin, is presented obliquely, but, unlike Dublin, with only occasional place names. An upland road, a hospital, a piazza, a market appear deliberately unidentified, yet they come into being as the girl or her family passes through them. The city is made recognizable with its up and down streets, the brown overlapping tiles of its roofs, the Cimitero Israelitico, the nationalistic chafing at Austro-Hungarian rule. Against it are counterposed images not only of Paris, as in *Ulysses*, but also of Padua and of the rice country near Vercelli. Through these continental scenes Giacomo moves, foreign and desirous. As a character he is older and less arrogant than Stephen, younger and more purposeful than Bloom, a middle son in their literary family.

The manuscript is not dated, but it describes a series of slender occurrences and swollen emotions that must have absorbed Joyce's mind over many months. Several events which are mentioned can be dated. For example, at the Jewish cemetery Giacomo is in the company of 'pimply Meissel', who has come to mourn at his wife's grave. This was Filippo

Meissel, whose wife, Ada Hirsch Meissel, committed suicide on 20 October 1911. Another indication of time is a reference to the expulsion of a music critic named Ettore Albini from La Scala in Milan, because he failed to stand when the 'Marcia Reale', anthem of the Kingdom of Italy, was played. Albini, who wrote for the Roman socialist newspaper *Avanti!* rather than, as Joyce says, for the Turin daily *Il Secolo*, was expelled on 17 December 1911, at a benefit concert for the Italian Red Cross and the families of soldiers killed or wounded in Libya, where Italy was fighting the Turks. A description of Padua at night must derive from Joyce's two trips to that city late in April 1912, when he went to be examined in the hope of qualifying to teach English at an Italian high school. The rice field near Vercelli which he remarks upon would be visible from the train between Milan and Turin; he took this route on his way to Ireland in July 1912. There is also an allusion to his lectures on *Hamlet* 'to docile Trieste'. These lectures took place from November 1912 to February 1913.

The fact that he shows his pupil at least some of *A Portrait of the Artist as a Young Man* extends the composition of *Giacomo Joyce* to a still later date. In June 1914, Joyce had the third chapter of his manuscript typed so that he could send it to the *Egoist* in London, where the novel was being serialized. At that time he evidently had other copies made, for he lent one to his friend Italo Svevo, and he indicates that he lent another to his pupil. He was then still working on the last two of the book's five chapters. While Joyce probably relied to some extent on earlier notes, he could not have written *Giacomo Joyce* down as a whole before the end of June 1914.

He cannot have deferred it for long after that, because Chapter V of *Portrait*, which he completed by 11 November 1914, contains from start to finish direct borrowings from *Giacomo Joyce*. Some are verbatim; most are reworked, such as the passage, 'My words in her mind: cold polished stones sinking through a quagmire', which becomes, in *Portrait*, 'The heavy lumpish phrase sank slowly out of hearing like a stone through a quagmire'. It seems probable that at some time before mid-November 1914 he had decided not to publish *Giacomo Joyce*, but to borrow from his manuscript for *Portrait* and *Ulysses*, and for his play, *Exiles*.

The painful misgivings of an ageing man are presented in *Giacomo Joyce* through a series of at once lush and sterile encounters. These take place at different spatial levels, always confirming distance. The pupil is conspicuously higher, 'a young person of quality' in her comfortable house up the hilly via Alice. Wrapped in odorous furs, herself strangely odourless, she stares through a lorgnette, tapping high heels, while he is below, eyeing 'upward from night and mud'. Once, at the opera, he sits above her, but there his position is even more inferior, for he is in the top gallery, surrounded by the plebeians and their smells, and, himself unseen, he gazes down at her cool small beauty, her green-dressed body and pinnacled hair below among the expensive people.

In the course of these shifting perspectives, Joyce unfolds the paradigm of unsatisfied love as it takes hold of the no longer young. Giacomo records the different inflections of his desire: he admires and sympathizes with his pupil, patronizes and secretly mocks her, hints, holds back, fails to speak out, succumbs like Stephen and Bloom to morose delectation, and describes with searing expertness his ludicrous unsuccess. The language shifts at moments to Shakespeare's diction, applied not only to love's tenderness but to 'pox-fouled wenches', and evokes with that diction an atmosphere of castles, princely hesitation, blazonry, court proprieties, Polonius with his daughter; but then it quickly diverges to two manners of Joyce's own, the coiling of words upon themselves in enwound repetition, to follow the 'curve of an emotion', as in much of *Portrait*, and the newer manner he was evolving for *Ulysses*, of sharp, certain, shorthand phrases which need no signalled emphasis.

From the beginning, when the pupil emerges out of nowhere to make him question, 'Who?', she is remote, pale, impalpable, removed from him by her glasses, by her cobweb handwriting, by her Jewishness, by her sheltered rearing, by her natural distinction, by her insurmountable virtue. Often the scene is misted, cloudy, vaporous, surrounded by ghosts at various degrees of manifestation, as if to envelop in an ominous and even deadly uncertainty both her and his passion for her.

And yet, among the clouds, he does not fail to summon up his pupil's distinctive being, her disconcerted recoils from his timid onslaughts, her fatigued delicacy, her intellectual ambition, her unceasing desirability. In the last pages the situation becomes hallucinatory; dream images thicken. He has fathomed her essence so completely that their eyes have intermingled. For a moment, like Robert Hand in *Exiles*, he dreams that she has been his, a fleeting sexual fantasy that nevertheless leaves him with a purpose: 'What then? Write it, damn you, write it! What else are you good for?'

After Joyce had brought himself to copying *Giacomo Joyce*, he had next to bring himself not to publish it. Since it was so open about his frailties, so little impersonalized (even if ironically detached) as to play truant from the aesthetic school just opened by Stephen Dedalus, Joyce was perhaps the readier to consider its abandonment. Yet he evidently liked *Giacomo Joyce* too much to sacrifice it before he had stamped his approval by making a fair copy.

Joyce also signalled approval by disseminating elements of *Giacomo Joyce* throughout his work. Its heroine, whom Giacomo relates to Dante's Beatrice and Shelley's Beatrice

Cenci, is related also to Beatrice Justice in *Exiles*. This Beatrice has similarly weak eyes – surrounded by beautiful lashes – with which she too has read the hero's earlier writings. In the play's first act she explains why she has come to Richard's house, and the words she uses are almost the same as the only words spoken directly by Giacomo's pupil: 'Otherwise I could not see you.'

Feelings registered in *Giacomo Joyce* proved applicable also to *Portrait*. Stephen, pondering a line from Thomas Nashe, calls to his mind the age of Elizabeth:

Eyes, opening from the darkness of desire, eyes that dimmed the breaking east. What was their languid grace but the softness of chambering? And what was their shimmer but the shimmer of the scum that mantled the cesspool of the court of a slobbering Stuart. And he tasted in the language of memory ambered wines, dying fallings of sweet airs, the proud pavan: and saw with the eyes of memory kind gentlewomen in Covent Garden wooing from their balconies with sucking mouths and the poxfouled wenches of the taverns and young wives that, gaily yielding to their ravishers, clipped and clipped again.

The images he had summoned gave him no pleasure. They were secret and enflaming but her image was not entangled by them. That was not the way to think of her. It was not even the way in which he thought of her. Could his mind then not trust itself? Old phrases, sweet only with a disinterred sweetness like the figseeds Cranly rooted out of his gleaming teeth.

The first paragraph is only a little altered from *Giacomo Joyce*; the second repudiates the first, as do later sentences. Giacomo does not accomplish so explicit a repudiation; he need not debate his vocabularies, he merely shifts them as moods shift.

In *Ulysses* Joyce follows Giacomo's rather than Stephen's method. The clashing of dictions becomes, in fact, the device to replace, in Joyce's later work, the elaborate and faintly precious interleavings of coloured words. In the same way, the erratic, contorted introspection of *Giacomo Joyce* helps to deflect *Portrait* from third-person narrative to Stephen's first-person diary at the end of that book, and prepares for the interior monologues of Bloom and Stephen.

As he came to *Ulysses*, Joyce took sentences from *Giacomo Joyce* and made them into whole paragraphs or longer units. Some slipped easily from work to work: morning in Trieste became morning in Paris, to be observed by Stephen more rancorously than was its correlative by Giacomo. A twilight image of mother and daughter as a mare and her fillyfoal is made entirely and beautifully equine for 'Oxen of the Sun'. The confrontation of Irishman and Jew is primarily a matter of male friendship rather than of heterosexual amorousness, and instead of lamenting the ageing process with Giacomo, Joyce apportions middle age to Bloom and youth to Stephen. Some of the scenes – the classroom, the graveyard, the Paduan brothels – are imported from the Adriatic to the Liffey. Oliver St John Gogarty, eternal antagonist, who makes a brief dream-visit to Giacomo in Trieste, turns up again in Dublin as Mulligan. *Giacomo Joyce* and *Ulysses* both contain Circean images of the unconscious, where the double sense of misbehaviour and compunction reaches a phantasmagoric climax.

Much later in the composition of *Ulysses*, at the end of 1918, Joyce approached a brunette on a Zurich street and expressed his astonishment at her resemblance to a girl he had seen in Dublin. In his subsequent correspondence with Martha Fleischmann, he attached extraordinary consequence to the possibility that she might be Jewish. Apparently he was looking for a new, and of necessity Swiss, embodiment of that

Judaeo-Celtic composite he was infatuated with in Trieste. Martha Fleischmann in turn became a model for Gerty MacDowell in 'Nausicaa', which parodies the fantasy, entertained in *Giacomo Joyce*, of possession by long distance. On a shabby genteel level, Bloom attempts psychic seduction of Martha Clifford as well, by writing letters to her, and so mimics ironically Joyce's own use of a literary medium to achieve a similar occult goal. A good deal of Joyce's writing can be seen to allude, at least *sotto voce*, to his middle-aged romance. Yet he also infuses *Giacomo Joyce* with independent life, and it stands now on its own terms as a fascinating achievement.

R.E. and J.W.-F.

Giacomo Joyce

Who?[1] A pale face surrounded by heavy odorous furs. Her movements are shy and nervous. She uses quizzing-glasses.[2] *Yes*: a brief syllable.[3] A brief laugh. A brief beat of the eyelids.

Cobweb handwriting, traced long and fine with quiet disdain and resignation: a young person of quality.

I launch forth on an easy wave of tepid speech: Swedenborg,[4] the pseudo-Areopagite,[5] Miguel de Molinos,[6] Joachim Abbas.[7] The wave is spent.[8] Her classmate, retwisting her twisted body, purrs in boneless Viennese Italian: *Che coltura!*[9] The long eyelids beat and lift: a burning needleprick stings and quivers in the velvet iris.

High heels clack hollow on the resonant stone stairs. Wintry air in the castle, gibbeted coats of mail, rude iron sconces over the windings of the winding turret stairs. Tapping clacking heels, a high and hollow noise. There is one below would speak with your ladyship.

She never blows her nose. A form of speech: the lesser for the greater.

Rounded and ripened: rounded by the lathe of intermarriage[10] and ripened in the forcing-house of the seclusion of her race.[11]

A ricefield near Vercelli under creamy summer haze. The wings of her drooping hat shadow her false smile. Shadows streak her falsely smiling face, smitten by the hot creamy light, grey wheyhued shadows under the jawbones, streaks of eggyolk yellow on the moistened brow,[12] rancid yellow humour lurking within the softened pulp of the eyes.[13]

A flower given by her to my daughter. Frail gift, frail giver, frail blue-veined child.[14]

Padua far beyond the sea. The silent middle age, night, darkness of history sleep in the *Piazza delle Erde* under the moon. The city sleeps. Under the arches in the dark streets near the river the whores' eyes spy out for fornicators. *Cinque servizi per cinque franchi.*[15] A dark wave of verse, again and again and again.

> *Mine eyes fail in darkness, mine eyes fail,*
> *Mine eyes fail in darkness, love.*

Again. No more. Dark love, dark longing. No more. Darkness.

Twilight. Crossing the *piazza*. Grey eve lowering on wide sagegreen pasturelands, shedding silently dusk and dew. She follows her mother with ungainly grace, the mare leading her filly foal. Grey twilight moulds softly the slim and shapely haunches, the meek supple tendonous neck, the fine-boned skull.[16] Eve, peace, the dusk of wonder . . . . Hillo! Ostler! Hilloho![17]

Papa and the girls sliding downhill, astride of a toboggan: the Grand Turk and his harem. Tightly capped and jacketted, boots laced in deft crisscross over the flesh-warmed tongue,[18] the short skirt taut from the round knobs of the knees. A white flash:[19] a flake, a snowflake:

> *And when she next doth ride abroad*
> *May I be there to see!*[20]

I rush out of the tobacco-shop and call her name. She turns and halts to hear my jumbled words of lessons, hours, lessons, hours: and slowly her pale cheeks are flushed with a kindling opal light. Nay, nay, be not afraid!

Mio padre: she does the simplest acts with distinction. *Unde derivatur? Mia figlia ha una grandissima ammirazione per il suo maestro inglese.*[21] The old man's face, handsome, flushed, with strongly Jewish features and long white whiskers, turns towards me as we walk down the hill together. O! Perfectly said: courtesy, benevolence, curiosity, trust, suspicion, naturalness, helplessness of age, confidence, frankness, urbanity, sincerity, warning, pathos, compassion: a perfect blend. Ignatius Loyola, make haste to help me![22]

This heart is sore and sad. Crossed in love?

Long lewdly leering lips: dark-blooded molluscs

Moving mists on the hill as I look upward from night and mud. Hanging mists over the damp trees. A light in the upper room. She is dressing to go to the play. There are ghosts in the mirror . . . . . Candles! Candles![23]

A gentle creature. At midnight, after music, all the way up the via San Michele, these words were spoken softly. Easy now, Jamesy! Did you never walk the streets of Dublin at night sobbing another name?

Corpses of Jews lie about me rotting in the mould of their holy field. Here is the tomb of her people, black stone, silence without hope . . . . . Pimply Meissel[24] brought me here. He is beyond those trees standing with covered head at the grave of his suicide wife, wondering how the woman who slept in his bed has come to this end . . . . . The tomb of her people and hers: black stone, silence without hope: and all is ready. Do not die!

She raises her arms in an effort to hook at the nape of her neck a gown of black veiling. She cannot: no, she cannot. She moves backwards towards me mutely. I raise my arms to help her: her arms fall. I hold the websoft edges of her gown and drawing them out to hook them I see through the opening of the black veil her lithe body sheathed in an orange shift.[25] It slips its ribbons of moorings at her shoulders and falls slowly: a lithe smooth naked body shimmering with silvery scales. It slips slowly over the slender buttocks of smooth polished silver and over their furrow, a tarnished silver shadow . . . . Fingers, cold and calm and moving . . . . A touch, a touch.[26]

Small witless helpless and thin breath. But bend and hear: a voice. A sparrow under the wheels of Juggernaut, shaking shaker of the earth. Please, mister God, big mister God! Goodbye, big world! . . . . *Aber das ist eine Schweinerei!*[27]

Great bows on her slim bronze shoes: spurs of a pampered fowl.[28]

The lady goes apace, apace, apace[29] . . . . . Pure air on the upland road. Trieste is waking rawly: raw sunlight over its huddled browntiled roofs, testudoform; a multitude of prostrate bugs await a national deliverance. Belluouro rises from the bed of his wife's lover's wife: the busy housewife is astir, sloe-eyed, a saucer of acetic acid in her hand[30] . . . . . Pure air and silence on the upland road: and hoofs.[31] A girl on horseback. Hedda! Hedda Gabler![32]

The sellers offer on their altars the first fruits: green-flecked lemons, jewelled cherries, shameful peaches with torn leaves.[33] The carriage passes through the lane of canvas stalls, its wheel-spokes spinning in the glare.[34] Make way! Her father and his son sit in the carriage. They have owls' eyes and owls' wisdom. Owlish wisdom stares from their eyes brooding upon the lore of their *Summa contra Gentiles*.[35]

She thinks the Italian gentlemen were right to haul Ettore Albini, the critic of the *Secolo*, from the stalls because he did not stand up when the band played the Royal March.[36] She heard that at supper. Ay. They love their country when they are quite sure which country it is.[37]

She listens: virgin most prudent.[38]

A skirt caught back by her sudden moving knee; a white lace edging of an underskirt lifted unduly; a leg-stretched web of stocking.[39] *Si pol?*[40]

I play lightly, softly singing, John Dowland's languid song. *Loth to depart:*[41] I too am loth to go. That age is here and now. Here, opening from the darkness of desire, are eyes that dim the breaking East, their shimmer the shimmer of the scum that mantles the cesspool of the court of slobbering James. Here are wines all ambered, dying fallings of sweet airs, the proud pavan, kind gentlewomen wooing from their balconies with sucking mouths, the pox-fouled wenches and young wives that, gaily yielding to their ravishers, clip and clip again.[42]

In the raw veiled spring morning faint odours float of morning Paris: aniseed, damp sawdust, hot dough of bread: and as I cross the Pont Saint Michel the steelblue waking waters chill my heart.[43] They creep and lap about the island whereon men have lived since the stone age . . . . . Tawny gloom in the vast gargoyled church. It is cold as on that morning: *quia frigus erat.*[44] Upon the steps of the far high altar, naked as the body of the Lord, the ministers lie prostrate in weak prayer. The voice of an unseen reader rises, intoning the lesson from Hosea. *Haec dicit Dominus: in tribulatione sua mane consurgent ad me. Venite et revertamur ad Dominum*[45] . . . . She stands beside me, pale and chill, clothed with the shadows of the sindark nave,[46] her thin elbow at my arm. Her flesh recalls the thrill of that raw mist-veiled morning, hurrying torches, cruel eyes. Her soul is sorrowful, trembles and would weep.[47] Weep not for me, O daughter of Jerusalem![48]

I expound Shakespeare to docile Trieste:[49] Hamlet, quoth I, who is most courteous to gentle and simple is rude only to Polonius. Perhaps, an embittered idealist, he can see in the parents of his beloved only grotesque attempts on the part of nature to produce her image[50] . . . . Marked you that?[51]

She walks before me along the corridor and as she walks a dark coil of her hair slowly uncoils and falls.[52] Slowly uncoiling, falling hair! She does not know and walks before me, simple and proud.[53] So did she walk by Dante in simple pride and so, stainless of blood and violation, the daughter of Cenci, Beatrice,[54] to her death:

> . . . . *Tie*
> *My girdle for me and bind up this hair*
> *In any simple knot.*[55]

The housemaid tells me that they had to take her away at once to the hospital, *poveretta*, that she suffered so much, so much, *poveretta*, that it is very grave . . . . . . I walk away from her empty house. I feel that I am about to cry. Ah, no! It will not be like that, in a moment, without a word, without a look. No, no! Surely hell's luck will not fail me!

Operated. The surgeon's knife has probed in her entrails and withdrawn, leaving the raw jagged gash of its passage on her belly. I see her full dark suffering eyes, beautiful as the eyes of an antelope.[56] O cruel wound! Libidinous God!

Once more in her chair by the window, happy words on her tongue, happy laughter. A bird twittering after storm, happy that its little foolish life has fluttered out of reach of the clutching fingers of an epileptic lord and giver of life, twittering happily, twittering and chirping happily.

She says that, had *The Portrait of the Artist* been frank only for frankness' sake, she would have asked why I had given it to her to read. O you would, would you? A lady of letters.[57]

She stands black-robed at the telephone. Little timid laughs, little cries, timid runs of speech suddenly broken . . . . *Parlerò colla mamma*[58] . . . . Come! chook, chook! come![59] The black pullet is frightened: little runs suddenly broken, little timid cries: it is crying for its mamma, the portly hen.

Loggione.[60] The sodden walls ooze a steamy damp.[61] A symphony of smells fuses the mass of huddled human forms: sour reek of armpits,[62] nozzled oranges, melting breast ointments,[63] mastick water,[64] the breath of suppers of sulphurous garlic, foul phosphorescent farts, opoponax,[65] the frank sweat of marriageable and married womankind, the soapy stink of men . . . . . . All night I have watched her, all night I shall see her: braided and pinnacled hair and olive oval face and calm soft eyes. A green fillet upon her hair and about her body a green-broidered gown: the hue of the illusion of the vegetable glass of nature and of lush grass, the hair of graves.[66]

My words in her mind: cold polished stones sinking through a quagmire.[67]

Those quiet cold fingers have touched the pages, foul and fair, on which my shame shall glow for ever. Quiet and cold and pure fingers. Have they never erred?

Her body has no smell: an odourless flower.

On the stairs. A cold frail hand: shyness, silence: dark langour-flooded eyes: weariness.[68]

Whirling wreaths of grey vapour upon the heath. Her face, how grey and grave! Dark matted hair. Her lips press softly, her sighing breath comes through.[69] Kissed.

My voice, dying in the echoes of its words, dies like the wisdom-wearied voice of the Eternal calling on Abraham through echoing hills. She leans back against the pillowed wall: odalisque-featured in the luxurious obscurity.[70] Her eyes have drunk my thoughts: and into the moist warm yielding welcoming darkness of her womanhood my soul, itself dissolving, has streamed and poured and flooded a liquid and abundant seed[71] . . . . . . Take her now who will! . . . .

As I come out of Ralli's house[72] I come upon her suddenly as we both are giving alms to a blind beggar. She answers my sudden greeting by turning and averting her black basilisk eyes.[73] *E col suo vedere attosca l'uomo quando lo vede.* I Thank you for the word, messer Brunetto.[74]

They spread under my feet carpets for the son of man. They await my passing. She stands in the yellow shadow of the hall,[75] a plaid cloak shielding from chills her sinking shoulders: and as I halt in wonder and look about me she greets me wintrily and passes up the staircase darting at me for an instant out of her sluggish sidelong eyes a jet of liquorish venom.[76]

A soft crumpled peagreen cover drapes the lounge. A narrow Parisian room. The hairdresser lay here but now. I kissed her stocking and the hem of her rustblack dusty skirt. It is the other. She. Gogarty came yesterday to be introduced. *Ulysses*

is the reason. Symbol of the intellectual conscience . . . .
Ireland then?[77] And the husband? Pacing the corridor in list
shoes or playing chess against himself. Why are we left here?
The hairdresser lay here but now, clutching my head between
her knobby knees . . . . Intellectual symbol of my race.[78]
Listen! The plunging gloom has fallen. Listen!
– I am not convinced that such activities of the mind or body
can be called unhealthy –
She speaks. A weak voice from beyond the cold stars.[79]
Voice of wisdom. Say on! O, say again, making me wise! This
voice I never heard.[80]
She coils towards me along the crumpled lounge. I cannot
move or speak. Coiling approach of starborn flesh.[81] Adultery
of wisdom. No. I will go. I will.
– Jim, love! –[82]
Soft sucking lips kiss my left armpit: a coiling kiss on myriad
veins. I burn! I crumple like a burning leaf! From my right
armpit a fang of flame leaps out.[83] A starry snake has kissed
me: a cold nightsnake.[84] I am lost!
– Nora! –

Jan Pieters Sweelink. The quaint name of the old Dutch
musician makes all beauty seem quaint and far. I hear his
variations for the clavichord on an old air: *Youth has an
end.*[85] In the vague mist of old sounds a faint point of light
appears: the speech of the soul is about to be heard. Youth has
an end: the end is here.[86] It will never be. You know that well.
What then? Write it, damn you, write it! What else are you
good for?

"Why?"
"Because otherwise I could not see you."[87]
Sliding – space – ages – foliage of stars – and waning heaven –
stillness – and stillness deeper – stillness of annihilation – and
her voice.[88]

Non hunc sed Barabbam![89]

Unreadiness. A bare apartment. Torbid [?Torpid] daylight. A
long black piano: coffin of music.[90] Poised on its edge a
woman's hat, red-flowered, and umbrella, furled.[91] Her arms:
a casque, gules, and blunt spear[92] on a field, sable.[93]

Envoy: Love me, love my umbrella.

PART III

Notes
and Index of Titles
and First Lines

Abbreviations and References

James Joyce's Manuscripts and Letters at the University of Buffalo: A Catalogue, compiled by Peter Spielberg, University of Buffalo, Buffalo, 1962.

The Cornell Joyce Collection: A Catalogue, compiled by Robert Scholes, Cornell University Press, Ithaca, 1961.

The Critical Writings of James Joyce, ed. Ellsworth Mason and Richard Ellmann, Faber and Faber, London; Viking Press, New York, 1959.

Dubliners, ed. Robert Scholes in consultation with Richard Ellmann, Viking Press, New York, 1967. (The text in the Viking Critical Library has the same pagination.)
In the notes page references to this edition are followed by the page numbers in the current British edition (Granada, 1977).

Exiles, Viking Press, New York, 1951.

Finnegans Wake, Faber and Faber, London; Viking Press, New York, 1939. (These editions have identical pagination.)

Ellmann, Richard, *James Joyce*, Oxford University Press, New York, London, 1982.

Letters of James Joyce, Vol. I, ed. Stuart Gilbert, Faber and Faber, London; Viking Press, New York, 1957; reissued with corrections, 1966. Vols. II and III, ed. Richard Ellmann, Faber and Faber, London; Viking Press, New York, 1966.

Joyce, Stanislaus, *My Brother's Keeper*, Faber and Faber, London; Viking Press, New York, 1958.
In the notes page references to this edition are followed by the page numbers in the Faber edition.

A Portrait of the Artist as a Young Man, ed. Chester G. Anderson in consultation with Richard Ellmann, Viking Press, New York, 1964. (The text in the Viking Critical Library has the same pagination.)
In the notes page references to this section are followed by the page numbers in the current British edition (Granada, 1977).

Stephen Hero, ed. John J. Slocum and Herbert Cahoon, New Directions, New York, 1944, 1963.
In the notes page references to this edition are followed by the page numbers in the current British edition (Granada, 1977).

John J. Slocum and Herbert Cahoon, *A Bibliography of James Joyce*, Yale University Press, New Haven, 1953.

Ulysses, Bodley Head and Penguin, London; Random House, New York, 1986.
In the notes the references to *Ulysses* begin with the episode and line numbers in the new and corrected edition, *e.g.* 3.411. These are followed by the page numbers for the 1961 Random House edition and the 1971 Penguin edition, since the older texts are still widely used and are cited in all criticism published before 1984.

A Note on the Text
of the Poems

On the basis of Richard Ellmann's transcriptions, collations and notes, it is possible to obtain a good sense of the editorial principles that governed his selection of texts. In general he relied on the last text that Joyce wrote or approved, although occasionally he followed his own taste in selecting another text (the 1907 first edition of *Chamber Music* was chosen because its punctuation and styling preserve the flavour of the early poems). In those cases where the manuscripts or typescripts have survived he made use of them (most of this material will be found in the Garland Press *Joyce Archive*; we have checked all these texts against the originals). In many instances, especially those involving the occasional poems, no authentic original is available, and we must rely on the transcriptions or memories of Joyce's acquaintances. Here Ellmann used his unmatched knowledge of the Joyce world in making his decisions.

Poems that appear in Joyce's fiction have not been included in this volume, since they depend upon their original contexts. The one exception to this policy is the 'Villanelle of the Temptress' that Stephen Dedalus composes in Chapter v of *A Portrait of the Artist as a Young Man*. According to Stanislaus Joyce (MBK 85–6/100–1), this poem was written by his brother during the *Shine and Dark* period (*c.* 1900), and we have printed it with the other youthful poems.

Those interested in the sources of the poems and epiphanies will find detailed information in Jacques Aubert's edition of *Oeuvres*, Volume One, and in the *Joyce Archive* (especially Volume One, *Poems*). Further information on the occasional poems is available in Paul A. Doyle's inventory of 'Joyce's Miscellaneous Verse', *James Joyce Quarterly*, 2 (1965), 90–6 and 5 (1967), 71. In the following notes we have recorded textual variants when they have a special critical interest, but our main aim has been to provide useful background information, identifications of allusions, and cross-references to Joyce's other works.

Chamber Music

Chamber Music was mainly the work of the years 1901–4. Joyce's brother Stanislaus told William York Tindall that Poem II belonged to an earlier collection, and it is transcribed in one of Stanislaus's notebooks under the title 'Commonplace' (Cornell 16). This was the title of one of the poems Joyce sent to William Archer in the summer of 1901 (*JJ* 83). By late 1902 Joyce had a substantial collection of poems in hand, which impressed Yeats and Arthur Symons. On 15 December 1902, shortly before returning to Dublin from Paris, he sent his friend J. F. Byrne a postcard with a Latin-Quarter photograph of himself and the final text of Poem XXXV, 'All day I hear the noise of waters'. The poem is headed 'Second Part – Opening which tells of the journeyings of the soul', an indication that Joyce had in mind a two-part series of poems on innocence and experience, rather like *Shine and Dark*. Joyce continued to write and revise poems through the emotionally charged years 1903–4. The fragment of Poem XXI written on the stationery of 'The Tower, Sandycove' places that poem in September 1904; the versions of Poems XXI and XXVII now at University College, Dublin, are also dated September 1904. Poem XXI may have been the last of the *Chamber Music* poems to be written, and as we shall see below it played a special role in the evolution of Joyce's verse-sequence. After the autumn of 1904 Joyce was concerned only with the arrangement of the volume, as it passed through the hands of four publishers before being issued by Elkin Mathews in May 1907.

The earliest manuscript of the *Chamber Music* suite, formerly in the collection of James Gilvarry and now owned by the University of Tulsa, closely resembles the manuscript that Joyce read from when he first met Oliver St John Gogarty in 1903. 'In the middle of each page was a little lyric that looked all the more dainty from the beautiful handwriting in which it was written; Tennysonian, exquisite things' (Gogarty, *Mourning Became Mrs Spendlove*, New York, 1948, p. 42).

The twenty-seven poems in the first Gilvarry sequence are written neatly in the centre of large sheets, and numbered 1 to 27 in this order: I, III, II, IV, V, VIII, VII, IX, XVII, XVIII, VI, X, XIII, XIV, XV, XIX, XXIII, XXII, XXIV, XVI, XXXI, XXVIII, XXIX, XXXII, XXX, XXXIII, XXXIV. The second sequence consists of Poems XXVII, XI, XII, XXVI and XXV, numbered 1–5, and Poem XX, which is numbered 13 (this would be its place in the 1905 Yale sequence if the programme piece, XXI, were omitted).

Two fuller *Chamber Music* sequences are Cornell 21 and the 1905 Yale manuscript (Slocum E.1.b). The thirty-one poems at Cornell were probably collected by Stanislaus in 1902–4, given their first arrangement in 1904–5, and then rearranged by him in 1906 (see below).

The line of transmission involving the Gilvarry, Cornell 21 and Yale (1905) manuscripts is difficult to determine. For example, line 10 of Poem XXIII, which reads 'Where love sighs not from sleep to sleep' in the Gilvarry manuscript, is crossed out in the Cornell manuscript and 'Folded in fragrant gloom asleep' is substituted in another hand. This revised line is also found in the Yale (1905) sequence, but in the 1906 fair copy Joyce reverts to the Gilvarry version. (This line was altered again on the 1907 page proofs.)

The Yale (1905) sequence has on its title page the address in Trieste where Joyce lived from 1 May 1905 to 24 February 1906. The order of the thirty-four poems at Yale is the original order of the Cornell sequence, which obviously represents a careful and long-considered plan: XXI, I, III, II, IV, V, VIII, VII, IX, XVII, XVIII, VI, X, XX, XIII, XI, XIV, XIX, XV, XXIII, XXIV, XVI, XXXI, XXII, XXVI, XII, XXVII, XXVIII, XXV, XXIX, XXXII, XXX, XXXIII, XXXIV. With a few exceptions in the middle poems, the Gilvarry sequence of twenty-seven poems corresponds to Yale (1905); and when the six other Gilvarry poems are included, they account for every poem in the Yale (1905) sequence except Poem XXI. Writing to Geoffrey Palmer on 19 July 1909 about the possibility of setting the poems to music, Joyce said: 'The book is in fact a suite of songs and if I were a musician I suppose I should have set them to music myself. The central song is XIV after which the movement is all downwards until XXXIV which is vitally the end of the book. XXXV and XXXVI are tailpieces just as I and III are preludes' (*L*,I,67). In the Gilvarry sequence I and III are the opening poems, XXXIV is the close, and XIV stands squarely in the middle, flanked by thirteen poems on either side. This symmetry of musical and emotional effects was spoiled slightly as Joyce added later poems, until finally in the rearrangement for the 1907 edition it was almost entirely obscured.

Poem XXI, the new programme piece for the Cornell and Yale (1905) sequences, was a response to Joyce's intense experiences in the summer of 1904. The third line of the earliest copy, written on the stationery of 'The Tower, Sandycove' (Cornell 23), reads: 'Amid his foes in scorn and wrath'. In Cornell 21 and Yale (1905) 'foes' is altered to 'friends', but the line returns to its original form in the 1906 fair copy. Richard Ellmann saw Poem XXI as a reflection of Joyce's break with Gogarty, his fear of betrayal, and his concern for Nora; the dedication 'To Nora' on Constantine Curran's copy of the poem, dated 30 September 1904, bears out this reading.

In the 1906 final manuscript, a fair copy with printer's instructions, Poem XXI is buried in the middle of the sequence, thereby restoring a more formal structure and tone to the suite. On 17 October 1906 Joyce wrote to Elkin

Mathews that he was 're-arranging' his verses and would send them on in a few days (L,II,180). In fact, Stanislaus played a decisive role in the rearrangement. In 1953 he wrote to William York Tindall:

The arrangment of the poems in 'Chamber Music' is not my brother's; it is mine. He sent the ms. to me from Rome, telling me 'to do what I liked with it'. He practically disowned the poems . . . I arranged them, now, in their present order – approximately allegretto, andante cantabile, mosso – to suggest a closed episode of youth and love . . .

My brother accepted my arrangement of his poems without question and without comment . . . In making my arrangement, I had, of course, in mind the last fateful year or so before he went into voluntary exile. I wished the poems to be read as a connected sequence, representing the closed chapter of that intensely lived life in Dublin, or more broadly, representing the withering of the Adonis garden of youth and pleasure.

(*Chamber Music*, ed. Tindall, New York, 1954, p. 44)

Stanislaus may be exaggerating somewhat, in characteristic fashion, and it is always dangerous to rely on memories of nearly a half-century before; but Joyce's letters bear out the claim. On 9 October 1906 he wrote to his brother: 'Tell me what arrangement you propose for the verses. I will follow it perfunctorily as I take very little interest in the publication of the verses' (L, II, 172). And when the proofs arrived from Elkin Mathews in late February 1907 Joyce marked up one copy and sent the other uncorrected copy (Cornell 24) to Stanislaus 'to see if the order is correct' (L, II, 219). Although Joyce did not accept Stanislaus's rearrangement of the poems without question, and did have enough interest to make changes on proof, it is certainly true that his enthusiasm for *Chamber Music* waned in the years 1904–7 as he became totally absorbed in the writing of *Dubliners*.

There is another very special manuscript of *Chamber Music* in a private collection. Joyce copied the thirty-six poems out in careful longhand on parchment and had them bound in beige leather with red horizontal bands with the monogram N. J. and the family arms engraved on the cover. The volume is inscribed 'To my darling, Nora, Christmas 1909'. The following has been added: 'This copy of my poems has been done by me in Dublin and completed on the 11th day of November 1909'.

II – Stanislaus Joyce placed this poem, originally entitled 'Commonplace', among the early poems of the *Shine and Dark* period (*MBK* 86/100–1). It was one of the poems that Joyce sent to William Archer, the translator of Ibsen, in the late summer of 1901 (*JJ* 83).
IV – This poem, along with XXXVI, was sent by Joyce from Paris to Stanislaus in Dublin on 8 Feb. 1903 (L, II, 28–29).
VII – Echoed in *The Holy Office*, line 71.

IX – Joyce had the last line engraved on a necklace which he presented to his wife in 1909.

XI – Dated 18 Sept. 1904 in a miscellaneous manuscript at Yale. Joyce set this poem to music.

XII – See Stanislaus Joyce's account of the origin of this poem quoted in the Introduction (*MBK* 150–1/157–9).

XIV – Joyce considered this the 'central song' in *Chamber Music* (*L*, I, 67).

XV – Written by 31 July 1904 as a 'matutine' to balance the nocturne in prose, 'She comes at night when the city is still' (Epiphany 34) (*The Dublin Diary of Stanislaus Joyce*, ed. George H. Healey, Cornell University Press, Ithaca, 1962, p. 62).

XVII – This poem apparently grew out of an incident described in Joyce's letter to Nora Barnacle of 15 Aug. 1904: 'I hear nothing but your voice. I am like a fool hearing you call me "Dear". I offended two men today by leaving them coolly. I wanted to hear your voice, not theirs' (*L*, II, 46). The 'friend' of the last line is almost certainly Oliver St John Gogarty (the model for Buck Mulligan in *Ulysses*), with whom Joyce was sharing the Martello Tower at Sandycove in the summer of 1904. For information on Joyce's 'break' with Gogarty, see *JJ* 174–5.

XX – The following is an early state of the poem dated 1903 (formerly in the possession of Stanislaus Joyce).

> In the dark pinewood
> There, O there,
> Beside you, dearest,
> I would I were!
>
> For the night is still there,
> Still and grave,
> Repose in the shadows
> Should we have.
>
> In the dark pinewood,
> There, O there,
> Beside you, dearest,
> I would I were!
>
> The kindly elves there
> To revel go,
> And peace, sweet peace there
> Should we know.

XXI – In one of Joyce's first arrangements this poem was prefatory and had the dedication 'To Nora', which on 11 June 1905 he decided to omit (*L*, II, 92).

XXVI – Joyce wrote to Nora on 21 Aug. 1909 about the woman for whom he had composed this poem and XXVIII: 'She was perhaps (as I saw her in my imagination) a girl fashioned into a curious grave beauty by the culture of generations before her' (*L*, II, 237).

XXVII – Written by 31 July 1904 but subsequently altered. In the original version the words 'Dearest' and 'Dearer' were 'used with the same accent at the beginning of two lines in the second verse', and the last couplet was needlessly recapitulatory (Stanislaus Joyce, *Dublin Diary*, p. 63). In the Gilvarry and University College, Dublin, manuscripts the last two lines read:

> But this I know – it scarce could be
> Dearer than is thy falsity.

XXIX – In the Gilvarry and Yale (1905) manuscripts lines 10–11 read:

> When over us the dark winds blow –
> But you, dear heart, too dear to me,

XXXIV – Of this poem Joyce wrote to the Irish composer G. Molyneux Palmer: ' "Sleep Now" is in its place at the end of the diminuendo movement and the two last songs are intended to represent the awakening of the mind. "O sleep *for* the winter etc" means "you had better sleep if you can because the winter will try to prevent you if *it* can" ' (*L*, I, 158). Joyce considered that after XIV 'the movement is all downwards until XXXIV which is vitally the end of the book' (*L*, I, 67).

XXXV – When Joyce sent a copy of this poem from Paris to J. F. Byrne on 15 Dec. 1902 he gave it the title: 'Second Part – Opening which tells of the journeyings of the soul' (*L*, II, 20). Joyce considered this and the following poem 'tailpieces' (*L*, I, 67).

XXXVI – An earlier version of this poem was sent from Paris to Stanislaus in Dublin on 8 Feb. 1903 (*L*, II, 28). Joyce said that it, like XXXV, was 'for the second part'. Ezra Pound included the poem in his *Des Imagistes* anthology of 1914.

Pomes Penyeach

The first poem, 'Cabra' (later 'Ruminants' and finally 'Tilly', the extra measure), was written shortly after the death of Joyce's mother in August 1903. Omitted from *Chamber Music* because it was out of key with the tone and subjects of that volume, 'Tilly' later joined company with twelve other intensely autobiographical poems written between 1912 and 1924.

The first numbered sequence of *Pomes Penyeach* is found in a Zurich notebook of *c.* 1918–19 (Buffalo IV.A.1). It includes all the poems except 'A Prayer' (written later in 1924) and 'A Memory of the Players in a Mirror at Midnight', which may have been unfinished at that time. With the writing of 'A Prayer' in spring 1924 the collection was completed, but Joyce did not publish it until mid-1927. There is some evidence that he published the poems as an answer to those friends, such as Harriet Weaver and Ezra Pound, who felt that he was losing himself in the obliquities of *Finnegans Wake*.

The final manuscript/typescript of *Pomes Penyeach*, now at the Huntington Library, assigns a place and date to each poem, as does the Shakespeare and Company first edition (the source of the present text). However, several changes were made in the process of publication, for reasons that are not entirely clear. The revised date for 'She Weeps Over Rahoon' (Trieste, 1913 instead of Trieste, 1914) moves that poem closer to the actual time of inspiration and composition, but the revised date for 'Watching the Needle-boats at San Sabba' (Trieste, 1912 instead of Trieste, 1913) is certainly too early. The changes may have been the product of inconsistencies in Joyce's memory, or they could have resulted from an attempt to give more coherence to the pattern of emotional development traced by the poems.

1 – 'Tilly'. The title means the thirteenth in a baker's dozen. The original title was 'Cabra', the name of the district in Dublin where Joyce's family lived; in 1919 this was changed to 'Ruminants'. Writing to Stanislaus on 18 Oct. 1906, Joyce asked his brother if he thought 'Cabra' should be included in *Chamber Music*. 'Can I use it here or must I publish it in a book by itself as, of course, my dancing days are over' (*L*, 11, 181).

The poem was written before 26 Sept. 1903 in its first form, since Stanislaus quotes it in his diary (p. 14). The early version (Cornell 54) reads:

Cabra

He travels after the wintry sun,
Driving his cattle along the straight red road,
Calling to them in a voice they know,
He drives the cattle above Cabra.

His voice tells them home is not far.
They low and make soft music with their hoofs.
He drives them without labour before him,
Steam pluming their foreheads.

O herdsman, careful of the herd,
Tonight sleep well by the fire
When the herd too is asleep
And the door made fast.

2 – 'Watching the Needleboats at San Sabba'. Joyce had seen his brother take part in a race of needleboats (racing shells) at San Sabba, near Trieste. As the scullers pulled towards shore, they began to sing an aria from the last act of Puccini's *La Fanciulla del West*.

> Aspettera ch'io torni . . .
> E passeranno i giorni,
> ed io non tornero . . .
>
> (Let her await my return.
> The days will pass away,
> and I shall not return.)

He sent the poem to his brother on 9 Sept. 1913 with the comment: 'I present the enclosed lines to your young friends of the *Rowing Club* if they want them for a dinner programme or some such thing – with the rheumatic chamber poet's (or pot's) compliments. *Quid si prisca redit Venus?* Perhaps you may like them' (*L*, II, 323–4). The Latin phrase 'What if the old love should return?' (i.e., 'What if I should begin to write verse again?') is taken from Horace, *Carmina* 3.9.17.

At the time of writing this poem Joyce was thirty-one, which he sometimes remarked was the end of what the Romans called *adulescentia*, or youth.

3 – 'A Flower Given to My Daughter'. This poem had its origin in an incident recorded in *Giacomo Joyce* (see p. 230). 'A flower given by her to my daughter. Frail gift, frail giver, frail blue-veined child.'

4 – 'She Weeps Over Rahoon'. In the notes to *Exiles* (pp. 117–18; 13 Nov. 1913) Joyce connects this poem with a friend of Nora's youth, Bodkin, who was the model for Michael Furey in 'The Dead'. Rahoon is the site of a cemetery in Galway.

Moon: Shelley's grave in Rome. He is rising from it: blond she weeps for him. He has fought in vain for an ideal and died killed by the world. Yet he rises. Graveyard at Rahoon by moonlight where Bodkin's grave is. He lies in the grave. She sees his tomb (family vault) and weeps. The name is homely. Shelley's is strange and wild. He is dark, unrisen, killed by love and life, young. The earth holds him. . . . She weeps over Rahoon too, over him whom her love has killed, the dark boy whom, as the earth, she embraces in death and disintegration. He is her buried life, her past. . . . She is Magdalen who weeps remembering the loves she could not return.

5 – 'Tutto è Sciolto'. This poem derives from the same amorous feelings as 'A Flower Given to My Daughter'. The Triestine pupil described in *Giacomo Joyce* had been mentally if not physically possessed, or at least Joyce seems to have thought so. The title is from Bellini's *La Sonnambula*, and is sung by Amina shortly after she has been discovered in Count Rodolpho's room (which she entered while sleepwalking). The phrase is translated 'All is lost now' in the English libretto. It is quoted several times in *Ulysses*, most notably in the 'Sirens' episode, where Bloom says to himself: 'Lovely air. In sleep she went to him . . . Yes: all is lost.' (11.638–41/272–3/271).

6 – 'On the Beach at Fontana'. In a Trieste notebook Joyce writes about his son George:

I held him in the sea at the baths of Fontana and felt with humble love the trembling of his frail shoulders: *Asperge me, Domine, hyssopo et mundabor: lavabis me et super nivem dealbalor.* [Thou shalt sprinkle me with hyssop, O Lord, and I shall be cleansed: thou shalt wash me and I shall be made whiter than snow].

(*The Workshop of Daedalus*, p. 99)

7 – 'Simples'. The epigraph is from a popular Italian song: 'O beautiful blond, / You are like the wave.' The child is Joyce's daughter Lucia.

8 – 'Flood'. Probably related to Joyce's love for his Triestine pupil.

9 – 'Nightpiece'. This poem is based on a scene in *Giacomo Joyce* where he enters the cathedral of Notre Dame in Paris on Good Friday (see p. 235).

11 – 'A Memory of the Players in a Mirror at Midnight'. This poem resulted from Joyce's involvement with the English Players, a group of amateur actors in Zurich (see *JJ* 423–8).

12 – 'Bahnhofstrasse'. Joyce had his first attack of glaucoma in the Bahnhofstrasse in Zurich in August 1917, and had to have an immediate operation.

13 – 'A Prayer'. The first poem Joyce had written in six years, this was sent to Valery Larbaud on 22 May 1924.

Ecce Puer

This poem ('Behold the young boy') simultaneously celebrates the birth of Joyce's grandson Stephen James Joyce (15 February 1932) and mourns the death of Joyce's father, John Stanislaus Joyce (29 December 1931). In several manuscript versions and one printing (*The Criterion*, Jan. 1933) the second line reads: 'A boy is born'.

Youthful Poems

All but the first three (see notes on them below) are found on the versos of the first thirty leaves in Stanislaus Joyce's commonplace book (Cornell 3). They date from *c.* 1900 and probably belong to Joyce's second collection *Shine and Dark*, although some poems from the first collection, *Moods*, may have been carried over. Most of the poems are incomplete because Stanislaus used only the lower halves of the pages upon which the poems had been written. We have indicated the breaks with rows of dashes, and have not provided conjectural readings of lines that are only partially visible.

'Et Tu, Healy'. Not long after the death of Charles Stewart Parnell on 6 Oct. 1891, the nine-year-old James Joyce wrote a poem denouncing those who had 'betrayed' Parnell. Like his father, the young Joyce considered the politician Tim Healy – who had been Parnell's close associate but later turned against him – a symbol for all those who abandoned their leader.

Joyce's father was so pleased with the poem that he had it printed and distributed to his friends. No copy of the broadside has survived; these two fragments are from Joyce's letter to Harriet Weaver of 22 Nov. 1930 (*L*, I, 295) and Stanislaus Joyce's *My Brother's Keeper* (46/65).

In *Finnegans Wake* II.1. Joyce's anti-self Shaun 'maunders off into sentimental poetry of what I actually wrote at the age of nine' (*L*, I, 295):

> *– My God, alas, that dear olt tumtum home*
> *Whereof in youthfood port I preyed*
> *Amook the verdigrassy convict vallsall dazes.*
> *And cloitered for amourmeant in thy boosome shede!*

> (*FW* 231)

'O fons Bandusiae'. A translation (made *c.* 1896) of Horace's ode (3.13) that opens: 'O fons Bandusiae splendidior vitro. . .'

'Are you not weary of ardent ways'. This is the poem that Stephen Dedalus composes in Chapter v of *A Portrait of the Artist as a Young Man* (223–4/ 202). Stanislaus called it 'The Villanelle of the Temptress' and dated it from the *Shine and Dark* period (*MBK* 85–6/100–1).

'A voice that sings'. A translation of Paul Verlaine's 'Chanson d'automne', which opens:

Les sanglots longs
Des violons
De l'automne
Blessent mon cœur
D'une langueur
Monotone.

'We will leave the village behind'. Dated Mullingar, July 1900, and described in Joyce's hand as 'A gypsy's song, in the third act of "A Brilliant Career".' In 1900 Joyce completed a prose play, *A Brilliant Career*, which was an elaborate story in the Ibsen manner of a young doctor's ambitions and achievements. It was severely criticized by William Archer, and Joyce destroyed the play in 1902. For a reconstruction of the plot (from Archer's letter of criticism and Stanislaus Joyce's memories) see *JJ* 78–80.

'Love that I can give you, lady'. Stanislaus Joyce (*MBK* 86/101) remembered the close of the last stanza:

To be listenin' to me mopin'
Here and singin', lady mine?

Joyce called the poem 'Rebuking', and when he asked Stanislaus what he thought of it, his brother told him 'in schoolboy fashion that . . . it was very nice but that he ought to change the "b" of the title into "p". [Joyce] laughed, but he wrote no more poems in the vernacular style . . .' (*MBK* 86–7/101).

'In the soft nightfall'. On the manuscript Joyce describes this poem as 'from an unfinished play "Dream Stuff".' We know that the play was in verse, and that 'In the soft nightfall' is all that survives.

Poems from the *Chamber Music* Cycle

These date from *c*. 1902–3. The poem which opens 'O, it is cold and still' was copied out by J. F. Byrne on library slips in March 1902. It bears the inscription 'dictated to J. F. B. Nat. Library, Dublin'. The variant beginning 'She is at peace where she is sleeping' is at Cornell (21b).

Of the poems which accompanied the *Chamber Music* manuscript now at Cornell, two listed by Robert Scholes (Cornell 21c and 21d) can no longer be located in the collection. Fortunately, 21c ('I said: I will go down to where') is duplicated by Cornell 12, and Richard Ellmann preserved a transcription of the missing 21d ('Alas, how sad the lover's lot').

The Holy Office

Joyce wrote this satirical broadside about two months before he left Dublin in October 1904. He had it printed but could not afford to pay for it, so the following year, in Pola, he had it printed again and sent the sheets to his brother Stanislaus for distribution in Dublin. In the poem he lumps together Yeats and George Russell and their followers, accusing them of hypocrisy and self-deception. The title refers ironically to (1) the office of confession and (2) the department of the Church that launched the Inquisition.

The following notes are keyed to line numbers.

4 – Joyce collected solecisms in the works of his eminent contemporaries.

24 – 'Mumming company' is used as a general derogatory label, but it is also a specific reference to the Abbey Theatre, which received its patent in August 1904.

25 – The 'him who hies him to appease' is Yeats.

26 – The 'giddy dames' are Lady Gregory, Annie Horniman (who sponsored the Abbey Theatre), and perhaps Maud Gonne.

28 – An allusion to the gilt decorations on the books Yeats published in the 1890s.

29–30 – The 'him who sober all the day / Mixes a naggin in his play' is John Millington Synge.

31–2 – Oliver St John Gogarty, who preferred a 'man of "tone".'

33–6 – The poet Padraic Colum.

37–40 – W. K. Magee ('John Eglinton'): see below, Occasional Poem 6.

41 – The 'him who loves his master dear' is George Roberts, a devoted follower of George Russell, who addressed Russell this way in a poem.

42 – James S. Starkey ('Seumas O'Sullivan'), who had witnessed Joyce's drunkenness: see below, Occasional Poem 9.

43–6 – George Russell.

57 – 'Though your sins be as scarlet, they shall be as white as snow.' Isaiah 1:18.

60 – A 'vicar-general' is a bishop's assistant who handles the operational details of the diocese.

74 – 'Leviathan' is the heroic Satan: here Joyce.

88 – 'There was his ground and he flung them disdain from flashing antlers' (*SH* 35/36).

94 – The Hindu great year.

Gas from a Burner

In September 1909 Joyce, then on a visit to Dublin, signed a contract with the firm of Maunsel and Co. to publish *Dubliners*. But George Roberts, the manager of the firm, began to find reasons for first delaying and then censoring the manuscript. Negotiations dragged along for three years, until finally Joyce returned to Dublin in 1912 and brought the matter to a head. Both Joyce and Roberts consulted solicitors; Roberts was advised that the use of actual names was libellous, and he began to demand so many changes that there was no possibility of agreement. Joyce left Dublin full of bitterness, which he vented by writing this broadside on the back of his contract with Maunsel and Co. while he was on the train between Flushing and Salzburg.

The following notes are keyed to line numbers.

19–20 – This incident actually took place in the summer of 1891, shortly before Parnell's death and after his 'betrayal' by former supporters.

24 – 'Billy Walsh' was His Grace the Most Reverend William J. Walsh, D.D., Archbishop of Dublin.

30 – 'Mountainy Mutton' was Joseph Campbell, author of *The Mountainy Singer* (published by Maunsel and Co. in 1909).

32 – The words 'bastard' and 'whore' are used in Campbell's *Judgment*, published by Maunsel in 1912.

33–6 – George Moore's play *The Apostle*, published by Maunsel in 1911.

38 – James Cousins, a Dublin theosophist and poet. The 'table book' is probably his *Etain the Beloved and Other Poems*, published by Maunsel in 1912.

42 – Maunsel published Lady Gregory's *Kiltartan History Book* in 1909 and *The Kiltartan Wonder Book* in 1910.

44 – 'What-do-you-Colm': Padraic Colum.

47 – The word 'shift', spoken by a character in Synge's *Playboy of the Western World*, caused a riot at the Abbey Theatre in 1907; Maunsel published the play in the same year.

48 – George Roberts was a traveller in ladies' underwear.

52 – O'Leary Curtis was a Dublin journalist; John Wyse Power was an official in the Royal Irish Constabulary in Dublin Castle (he figures in *Ulysses* as Jack Power and John Wyse Nolan).

53 – 'DEAR DIRTY DUBLIN', a phrase coined by Lady Sydney Morgan, is one of the newspaper captions in the 'Aeolus' episode of *Ulysses*.

54 – This line refers to Joyce's difficulty in finding a publisher for *Dubliners*.

60 – *The Origin and History of Irish Names of Places*, by Patrick Weston Joyce (no relation to James).

62 – 'Curly's Hole': a bathing pool at Dollymount, Clontarf.

64 – Roberts was an Ulster Scot, so Ireland is only his 'stepmother'. Roberts is the 'red-headed Scotchman' mentioned two lines later.

73 – The *Irish Review* was edited by Padraic Colum from March 1912 to July 1913.

85 – 'But I say unto you, That ye resist not evil: but whosoever shall smite thee on thy right cheek, turn to him the other also.' Christ in the Sermon on the Mount, Matthew 5:39.

98 – *Memento, homo, quia pulvis es* ('Remember, man, dust thou art'): the words of the priest on Ash Wednesday as he marks the cross of ashes on the communicant's forehead.

Occasional Poems

1 – 'G. O'Donnell'. George O'Donnell was a classmate of Joyce's at Belvedere College, and Joyce wrote this squib on the front page of O'Donnell's copy of P. W. Joyce's *A Concise History of Ireland*. The class 'had been reading Goldsmith's "Retaliation", and the sixteen-year-old Joyce singled out one of his classmates for an address that echoes Goldsmith's mock epitaphs' (Mary and Padraic Colum, *Our Friend James Joyce*, New York, 1958, p. 147).

'Murphies' are potatoes; Kilmainham was a jail in Dublin that had housed many Irish rebels and patriots; Drumcondra is a northern suburb of Dublin, a 'good address' in Joyce's time.

2 – 'There was on old lady named Gregory'. This limerick exists in various forms, as remembered by Joyce's friends. The version printed here is from Mary and Padraic Colum, *Our Friend James Joyce*, p. 12.

In November 1902, shortly before his first flight to Paris, Joyce wrote to Lady Augusta Gregory asking for assistance (*JJ* 107). She gave him friendly advice, and wrote some letters for him, but did not furnish him with what is referred to in *Ulysses* as 'some of the ready'.

3 – 'There was a young priest named Delaney'. Recorded by Oliver St John Gogarty in *Start from Somewhere Else* (New York, 1955), pp. 83–4. 'There was a Jesuit father, a convert, who, in spite of his name, was an Englishman. Joyce wrote to him from 4 Faithful Place, one of four or five houses that stood at the back of the red-light district of the city.'

4 and 5 – 'There is a weird poet called Russell' and 'A holy Hegelian Kettle'. In these poems recorded by Constantine Curran in *James Joyce Remembered* (London, 1968), p. 76, the targets are the Irish poet and theosophist George Russell (AE) and Joyce's friend of University College days Thomas Kettle (see *JJ* 62–3).

6 – 'John Eglinton, my Jo, John'. W. K. Magee, a member of the staff at the National Library, wrote graceful essays modelled on Matthew Arnold under the pen-name John Eglinton. He was a favourite butt of Joyce and Oliver Gogarty, who mocked his abstemious habits, and who evidently wrote this poem jointly. The blanks represent indecipherable words.

7 – 'Have you heard of the admiral, Togo'. According to Oliver St John Gogarty (*Start from Somewhere Else*, pp. 82–3), Joyce composed this limerick about the Japanese admiral Togo, who during the Japanese–Russian war refused shore leave to his sailors.

[263]

8 – 'There once was a Celtic librarian'. Another poem satirizing W. K. Magee ('John Eglinton').

9 – 'Dear, I am asking a favour'. A parody of a poem by 'Seumas O'Sullivan' (James S. Starkey), 'Praise', which begins:

> Dear, they are praising your beauty,
> The grass and the sky:
> The sky in a silence of wonder,
> The grass in a sigh.

10 – 'O, there are two brothers, the Fays'. Frank and William G. Fay were directors of the National Theatre Society. After the drunken Joyce was evicted from their theatre one night he banged his ashplant on the door and shouted: 'Open the door at once, Fay. You can't keep us out of your bawdy house. We know you' (*JJ* 160–1).

11 – 'The Sorrow of Love'. A parody of a poem with this title by 'Seumas O'Sullivan' (James S. Starkey), as recalled by Ulick O'Connor in *The Times I've Seen: Oliver St John Gogarty* (New York, 1963), p. 82.

The Sorrow of Love

> If I could tell the bright ones that
> quiet-hearted move
> . They would bend down like the branches
> with the sorrow of love.

12 – 'C'era una volta, una bella bambina'. A lullaby that Joyce used to rock his young daughter Lucia (b. 1907) to sleep.

> Once upon a time there was a beautiful little girl
> Who was called Lucia
> She slept all day
> She slept all night
> Because she did not know how to walk
> Because she did not know how to walk
> She slept all day
> She slept all night.

13 – 'The flower I gave rejected lies'. The manuscript of this poem (Cornell 50) is undated, but the mood fits the *Giacomo Joyce* period.

14 – 'There is a young gallant named Sax'. Victor Sax was a Zurich acquaintance who took lessons in English from Joyce. Once Joyce proposed that they write limericks for their daily lesson, and after overseeing Sax's productions Joyce produced this poem and the following one.

15 – 'There's a monarch who knows no repose'. This limerick is a parody of the Austro-Hungarian dual monarchy.

16 – 'Lament for the Yeomen'. An adaptation of 'Des Weibes Klage' by Felix Beran, a poet with whom Joyce was acquainted in Zurich. Joyce said it was the one good war poem that he knew. For the German text see *JJ* 431–2.

17 – 'There's a donor of lavish largesse'. This and the following limerick were sent to Claud W. Sykes on a postcard dated 5 Sept. 1917 (*L*, 11, 406). The donor is John Quinn, the New York lawyer and patron of the arts who generously supported Pound, Joyce, and other modern writers. He purchased the manuscripts of *Exiles* and *Ulysses*, and defended the *Little Review* in court when its editors were charged with 'obscenity' for publishing the 'Nausicaa' episode.

18 – 'There is a clean climber called Sykes'. Claud W. Sykes, one of Joyce's Zurich friends and language pupils, was keen on long walks and mountain climbing.

19 – 'There once was a lounger named Stephen'. Included in a letter to Ezra Pound of 9 April 1917 (*L*, 1, 102).

20 – 'Now let awhile my messmates be'. Included in a letter to Ezra Pound of 24 July 1917 (MS Yale).

21 – 'There once was an author named Wells'. In a highly appreciative review of *A Portrait of the Artist* (*Nation*, 24 Feb. 1917) H. G. Wells had complained that the hero, while intolerant of sounds, was singularly indulgent of smells.

22 – 'Solomon'. On a postcard to Claud W. Sykes dated 10 Sept. 1917 (*L*, 11, 406). Simeone Levi, one of Joyce's Zurich pupils, had come from Trieste, but Joyce somehow thought he was a Turkish subject.

23 – 'D. L. G.' On a postcard to Claud W. Sykes dated [November 1917] (*L*, 11, 410). The subject is David Lloyd George, British Prime Minister 1916–22.

24 – 'A Goldschmidt swam in a Kriegsverein'. Rudolf Goldschmidt, a well-to-do grain merchant in Zurich, took English lessons from Joyce and became a friend. He was an official in an organization which assisted Austro-Hungarian subjects resident in Switzerland. 'Kriegsverein' may be a play on (or mistake for) 'Kriegersverein', a 'group of warriors'. 'Schlachtfeld' was a battlefield in the First World War. The poem is to the tune of the 'Amorous Goldfish' in Sidney Jones's *The Geisha*.

25 – 'Dooleysprudence'. During the First World War Joyce was, from the point of view of British consular authorities in Switzerland, offensively neutral. He had remained in Trieste until the end of June 1915, when – to avoid internment – he moved to Switzerland. He gave his word to the Austrian officials that he would take no part in the war, and had no difficulty in keeping it. 'Dooleysprudence' reflects his pacifist irritation with both sides; its defence of the isolated exile recalls *The Holy Office*, but here as in *Ulysses* the hero is the common man.

The popular song 'Mr. Dooley' was written by Billy Jerome in 1901. The reference to 'income tax' in the fifth stanza recalls Joyce's refusal to pay three shillings and sixpence tax in Dublin in 1904.

26 – 'There's an anthropoid consul called Bennett'. A. Percy Bennett, the British Consul-General in Zurich (known to his colleagues as 'Pompous Percy'), treated Joyce in an offhand and superior way until needled by him, after which he lapsed into silence and pretended to be looking for something thrown by mistake into his waste-paper basket (*JJ* 425).

27 – 'New Tipperary'. Also called 'The C. G. Is Not Literary'. Joyce's complicated relationship with the English Players in Zurich is recounted in *JJ* 425–8, 439–41, and 445–7. One of the actors was Henry Carr, who worked at the British consulate. He and Joyce quarrelled over payment, and Joyce – always litigious – filed suit. Carr filed a counter-claim, asking among other things that he be reimbursed for the cost of his costume. Joyce saw his quarrel as a battle against British imperial power, and Consul-General Bennett (the 'C. G.') was soon involved. At one point Joyce even wrote to the Prime Minister to ask his help in the dispute with Consul-General Bennett. In the end Joyce won, and Carr had to pay court costs and reimburse Joyce for his trouble and expense. This poem celebrates the 'victory'.

The first play presented by the Players was Wilde's *The Importance of Being Earnest*. Carr is called 'Private Carr' because he let it be thought that he was an officer when in reality he was an ordinary soldier.

28 – 'To Budgeon, raughty tinker'. Frank Budgen, later the author of *James Joyce and the Making of 'Ulysses'* (1934), became Joyce's closest friend in Zurich. A self-educated Englishman who had studied painting in Paris, he and Joyce delighted in rowdy drinking parties, much to the disgust of Nora Joyce. At one of these parties Budgen sang 'The Raughty Tinker', which begins:

> There was a raughty tinker
> Who in London town did dwell . . .   (*JJ* 432)

Nora became reconciled to Budgen after she came to know him better, and her signature is at the bottom of this poem, along with Joyce's and those of two Zurich friends, Ethel Turner and W. H. Kerridge.

29 – 'A bard once in lakelapt Sirmione'. Ezra Pound, who had been supporting Joyce's work with typical generosity since 1914, finally met him on 8 June 1920. Joyce travelled from Trieste to Sirmione, on Lago di Garda, where Pound was staying. Since Joyce had written earlier of his need for clothing, Pound provided him with a suit and boots (which were too small). This transfer of clothing is memorialized in the limerick.

30 – 'The Right Heart in the Wrong Place'. On a postcard to Stanislaus Joyce dated 27 Aug. 1920 (*L*, III, 16). Joyce was stirred by the hunger strike of Terence MacSwiney, Lord Mayor of Cork, in Brixton Prison. MacSwiney was arrested on 12 Aug. 1920 for having a British cipher and other revolutionary

materials in his possession. His hunger strike lasted for 73 days and ended in his death on 25 Oct. 1920.

Sir Horace Rumbold was the British Minister in Berne to whom Joyce appealed unsuccessfully when the English Players in Zurich were boycotted by Consul-General Bennett.

31 – 'The Right Man in the Wrong Place'. On a postcard to Claud W. Sykes dated 27 Aug. 1920. Sir Horace Rumbold had been transferred to Warsaw as British Ambassador in 1919.

32 – 'O, Mr Poe'. In a letter to Ezra Pound dated 28 Sept. 1920 (MS Yale). 'I have also heard nothing either from the *Mercure* or from Mr Poe.' Joyce had hoped that Jacques Vallette, editor of the *Mercure de France*, would publish a French translation of *A Portrait of the Artist*, and that Aurélien-Marie Lugné-Poë, the actor and producer, would stage a French translation of *Exiles* at the Théâtre de l'Œuvre. Both projects came to nothing (see *JJ* 488, 497–8).

33 – 'Bis Dat Qui Cito Dat'. On a Christmas card to Ezra Pound dated 20 Dec. 1920 (*L*, III, 34). The title means 'He gives twice who gives quickly.' The poem probably refers to Richard Wallace, an American book illustrator in Paris who was trying to revive *The Little Review* (which had been closed down by the *Ulysses* trial). 'Inisfail' is a traditional name for Ireland.

34 – 'And I shall have no peace there for Joyce comes more and more'. This take-off on Yeats's 'The Lake Isle of Innisfree' ('And I shall have some peace there, for peace comes dropping slow') was probably written for Sylvia Beach during 1921, when Joyce was a frequent visitor to her bookshop as *Ulysses* neared publication.

35 – 'Who is Sylvia, what is she'. This adaptation of Shakespeare's 'Who is Sylvia? what is she' (from *The Two Gentlemen of Verona*), dated 13 February 1922, expresses Joyce's gratitude for Sylvia Beach's heroic efforts that led to the publication of *Ulysses* on his fortieth birthday, 2 February 1922.

36 – 'The press and the public misled me'. From a letter to Robert McAlmon of March 1922 which opens: 'Thanks for the ring and the ties. I don't mean you to go to Cannes to buy ties for me! God forbid. I thought you always travelled with a trunk full of them and threw out a few dozen a week but evidently I was misled by rumour' (*L*, I, 182). Robert McAlmon, the American poet and short-story writer living in Paris, became a close friend of Joyce in 1921–2 and was tireless in his help with the publication of *Ulysses*.

37 – 'Jimmy Joyce, Jimmy Joyce, where have you been?' In a letter sent to Harriet Shaw Weaver from Paris on 20 Sept. 1922. Joyce had returned from a few weeks in London, where he stayed in the Euston Hotel nursing his eyes.

38 – 'Fréderic's Duck'. This poem (dated 21 June 1923) memorializes an evening when Richard and Lillian Wallace took the Joyces to the famous restaurant La Tour d'Argent, described in a 1924 Baedeker of Paris as

'Frederick's Duck'. Frédéric, the original chef, died at the age of 70 sometime before 1913. To this day each duck served at the restaurant has a number.

39 – 'I never thought a fountain pen'. This little poem refers to the Richard Wallace of poems 33 and 38. 'Shem the Penman' is the autobiographical figure of the artist in *Finnegans Wake*.

40 – 'Rosy Brook he bought a book'. From a letter to Harriet Shaw Weaver of 24 May 1924, prefaced by the comment: 'Dr Rosenbach sent me a message asking me what would be my price for the corrected proofs of *Ulysses*. When he receives a reply from me all the rosy brooks will have run dry' (*L*, 1, 214). On 16 Jan. 1924 A. S. W. Rosenbach, the American book collector, purchased the manuscript of *Ulysses* at the John Quinn auction for $1975. Joyce was chagrined at the price, and wished to buy the manuscript back, but Rosenbach refused. He countered by cable with an offer to buy the corrected proofs. Rosebrook was the Rosenbach Company's cable address, and it seems likely that *Ulysses* was misspelled in the cable to Joyce.

41 – 'I saw at Miss Beach's when midday was shining'. From a letter to Sylvia Beach of 8 Nov. 1924, printed in *James Joyce's Letters to Sylvia Beach*, ed. Melissa Banta and Oscar A. Silverman (Indiana University Press, 1987), p. 51.

42 – 'Bran! Bran! The baker's ban!' Dated 5 April 1925 (MS Croessmann). During a bout of eye operations in spring 1925 Joyce was placed on a strict diet.

43 – 'P. J. T.' This limerick is about Patrick J. Tuohy, the Irish artist who painted portraits of Joyce and his father John Stanislaus.

44 – 'Post Ulixem Scriptum'. Dated on one version 12 March 1925, this celebration of Molly Bloom went through many revisions, and was the most carefully worked-over of all Joyce's occasional poems. 'Tim Healy' (line 3) is Timothy Michael Healy, the Irish politician who turned against Parnell and betrayed him (see the note on 'Et Tu, Healy' p. 257). 'Arrayed . . . for the bridal' (line 14) is the song that Aunt Julia sings in 'The Dead'. Leopold Bloom's family originally came from Hungary, and the picnic mentioned in the poem is the one Bloom recalls in *Ulysses*. Molly Bloom spent her youth in Gibraltar.

45 – 'The clinic was a patched one'. From a letter to Harriet Shaw Weaver of 25 April 1925 (*L*, 1, 227). 'I go to the clinic every morning [for treatment of his eyes] and rue de la Paix every evening. Do you know the poem *Little Jim* "The cottage was a thatched one". I rhyme it [this poem follows].'

46 – 'Is it dreadfully necessary'. From a letter to Harriet Shaw Weaver of 13 June 1925 (*L*, 1, 228). This parody of a canto by Ezra Pound is also headed '(With apologies to Miss Gertrude Stein)'.

47 – 'Rouen is the rainiest place getting'. This parody of T. S. Eliot's *The Waste Land* is in a letter to Harriet Shaw Weaver of 15 Aug. 1925 (*L*, 1, 231).

48 – 'There's a coughmixture scopolamine'. From a letter to Harriet Shaw

Weaver of 20 Jan. 1926 (*L*, I, 239). Scopolamine is a drug taken to dilate the pupil of the eye.

49 – 'Troppa Grazia, Sant' Antonio!' From a letter to Ezra Pound of [?8 Nov. 1927] (*L*, III, 166). In the letter the title is 'Troppa Grossa, San Giacomone!' The alternative title is found in a typescript version (Buffalo IV.B.4) dated 19 Nov. 1926.

50 – 'For he's a jolly queer fellow'. From a letter to Harriet Shaw Weaver of 1 Feb. 1927 (*L*, I, 249). The occasion was an International Protest against the pirated edition of *Ulysses* published by Samuel Roth in the USA.

51 – 'Scheveningen, 1927'. Dated Paris, 26 May 1927 (Buffalo IV.B.5). During a 1927 holiday Joyce spent much of his time on the beach near The Hague, while Sylvia Beach was losing money on *Ulysses*.

52 – 'Pour Ulysse IX'. From a typescript laid into one of Harriet Weaver's copies of *Ulysses*. The ninth episode of *Ulysses* is the Library episode dominated by Stephen Dedalus. 'Chandeleur' is Candlemas, 2 February, Joyce's birthday.

53 – 'Crossing to the Coast'. Dated Avignon 21 April 1928 (Buffalo IV.B.6).

54 – 'Hue's Hue? or Dalton's Dilemma'. Another hit at the pirating publisher Samuel Roth (Buffalo IV.B.7). John Dalton (1766–1844) first described colour blindness.

55 – 'Buried Alive'. A translation of a German poem, 'Lebendig Begraben', by Gottfried Keller. For the German text see Herbert Gorman, *James Joyce* (New York, 1948), p. 345.

56 – 'Father O'Ford'. Dated 16 Feb. 1930, this poem is about the novelist Ford Madox Ford who had taken an interest in Joyce's work. Joyce wrote to Harriet Weaver that Ford had recently appeared in Paris with a new wife, 'an eighth or eighteenth' (*JJ* 635).

57 – 'Buy a book in brown paper'. A dustjacket 'blurb' in the style of *Finnegans Wake* that Joyce wrote for the two-shilling Faber and Faber edition of *Anna Livia Plurabelle* (*FW* I.viii), which was published in June 1930.

58 – 'To Mrs H. G. who complained that her visitors kept late hours'. Mrs Herbert Gorman, the wife of Joyce's first biographer, complained to Joyce that her visitors, especially John Holms and Peggy Guggenheim, never wanted to leave.

59 – 'Humptydump Dublin squeaks through his norse'. A poem about Humphrey Chimpden Earwicker written as a 'blurb' for the Faber and Faber pamphlet *Haveth Childers Everywhere* (published May 1931). Joyce was a little annoyed when this blurb and the one for *Anna Livia Plurabelle* were only used in a mimeographed publicity release.

60 – 'Stephen's Green'. Translations of James Stephens's poem into French, German, Latin, Norwegian, and Italian. Joyce discusses the translations in a letter to Stephens of 7 May 1932 (*L*, I, 317–18).

61 – 'As I was going to Joyce Saint James'. This take-off on 'As I was going to St Ives' was recorded by Mary Colum in *Life and the Dream* (New York, 1947), p. 395. '[Joyce] wrote some verses on his women friends and their interference with him which he read to me with great gusto.'

62 – 'Pour la Rime Seulement'. The two writers involved in this poem are Valery Larbaud, who had played a major role in the launching of *Ulysses*, and Pierre Chardon de Lanux of *La Nouvelle Revue Française*, who was also a journalist accredited to the League of Nations.

63 – 'A Portrait of the Artist as an Ancient Mariner'. A poem about the vicissitudes of *Ulysses*, filled with allusions to the various difficulties in publication (see *JJ* 654–5). The Bull and Sam of stanza 2 are John Bull and Uncle Sam, who at this time (Oct. 1932) still banned *Ulysses*. 'K.O.11' is a knockout in the eleventh year since publication. The 'U. boat' (stanza 5) is *Ulysses*. 'Kugelkopfschwindel' (stanza 6) means 'dizziness'. White and blue (stanza 7) are the colours of the Greek flag and also of the first edition of *Ulysses*. Stanza 9 refers to the pirating of *Ulysses* in the USA and Japan; 'Albatross' was the press that took over publication of *Ulysses* in Europe from Sylvia Beach.

64 – 'Pennipomes Twoguineaseach'. Playing on *Pomes Penyeach*, these verses celebrate the publication of *The Joyce Book* (1933), a group of musical settings of Joyce's poems.

65 – 'There's a genial young poetriarch Euge'. A limerick about Eugene Jolas, founder of *transition* (which published Joyce's *Work in Progress*) and author of the manifesto 'The Revolution of the Word'. Joyce is playing on the title of Jolas's book *Mots Déluge*.

66 – 'Have you heard of one Humpty Dumpty'. Dated 5 Sept. 1933. The Magazine Wall in Phoenix Park, Dublin, is the site of HCE's fall in *Finnegans Wake*.

67 – 'Epilogue to Ibsen's "Ghosts" '. While Joyce never abandoned his early devotion to Ibsen, there is evidence in his last pronouncements that he thought some of Ibsen's techniques rather amusing. So in writing an epilogue to Ibsen's *Ghosts* in April 1934, after seeing the play performed, he out-Ibsens Ibsen by following up two devices, Spreading the Guilt and the Horrible Hint. Captain Alving points out that he is assumed to have fathered two children, one out of wedlock and one in, the first (Regina) healthy, the second (Oswald) congenitally sick. Pursuing the trail of guilt, and profiting from suggestions in *Ghosts* that Parson Manders and Mrs Alving were once in love, the captain wickedly implies that Manders was Oswald's father. He declares with equal effrontery that his own sins supplied incomparable material for a dramatic masterpiece.

The 'grim old grouser' of line 2 is Ibsen; the 'lewd knight in dirty linen' (line 6) is Falstaff in *The Merry Wives of Windsor*.

68 – 'Goodbye, Zurich, I must leave you'. In a letter sent from Zurich to

Giorgio and Helen Joyce, 28 Nov. 1934 (*L*, I, 352). It parodies a patriotic song, 'Dolly Gray', which opens: 'Good-bye, Dolly, I must leave you, / Though it breaks my heart to go.'

69 – 'Le bon repos'. On a letter-card sent to Stuart Gilbert on 1 July 1935 (*L*, I, 374–5). 'Des Espagneux' was the name of the villa on the shore of Lake Annecy where Gilbert was spending the summer.

70 – 'Aiutami dunque, O Musa, nitidissima Calligraphia!' From a letter to Giorgio Joyce of 28 Oct. 1935 (*L*, III, 379).

> Aid me then, O muse, resplendent Calligraphia!
> Supply the form and style, and curb the rebellious pen!
> Pour out limpid sound and distil the liquid sense,
> And over the parched sand, pray, extend your branch!
> (trans. Richard Ellmann)

71 – 'Come-all-ye'. Published in facsimile in *Pastimes of James Joyce* (New York, 1941) and dated 'Thanksgiving Day, 1937'. The Thanksgiving party had been at the Jolas home, and the fact that the turkey had been dropped on its way from the market, and had somehow lost its liver in the process, so diverted Joyce that he wrote this piece of light verse.

In the second stanza the Grand Palais Potin refers to Félix Potin, a grocery chain. 'Mujik' in stanza 7 was a faithful Russian servant who waited on table; 'Madamina' is the first word of an aria in *Don Giovanni* as well as a combination of 'Madame' (Jolas) and 'Balamina' (a Southern song she used to sing). The 'message from the Big Noise' was Franklin D. Roosevelt's Thanksgiving Day message.

72 – 'There's a maevusmarked maggot called Murphy'. From a manuscript pasted into Richard Ellmann's copy of Samuel Beckett's *Murphy*, and dated Paris, 30 April 1939.

Epiphanies

Of the forty surviving epiphanies, twenty-two are in Joyce's hand (Buffalo 1.A.) with numbers on the back that run from 1 to 71, indicating that there were at one time at least that many epiphanies or similar entries. The remaining epiphanies (Cornell 15, 17, 18) are copies made by Joyce's brother Stanislaus, with the exception of the final 'Gogarty' epiphany, which is a rough draft in Joyce's hand.

When Robert Scholes edited the epiphanies for *The Workshop of Daedalus* (Northwestern University Press, Evanston, 1965) he arranged them in chronological order, relying on both internal biographical evidence and the numbers on the versos of the twenty-two holograph leaves. We have followed his sequence and numbering, but have based the text on the original manuscripts.

Although some specific uses Joyce made of the epiphanies will be discussed in the notes to individual sketches, it seemed best to lay out all the major uses and echoes in tabular form.

	Stephen Hero	Portrait	Ulysses
1		8/7–8	
3	67–8/65	69–70, 71, 222/ 64, 71, 201	
5		68/63	17.139–41/ 670/590
6		137–8/126	
8	38/39		
9	251/219		
11	46/46		
12	43/44		
14	45/45		
15	244–5/213–14		
19	162–3/147		
21	167/150		6.517–20/101/ 103
22	169/152		
24		152/138	
25	183–4/165	216/196	
26		219/198	
27		251/226	
28		27/24	
29		249/225	
30	237/208–9	252/228	
31		100/92	
34			15.4195–204 /581/516 [also FW 193–4]
38			13.66–74/ 347/345

1 – With slight changes in its dramatic frame this epiphany became the powerful close to the first section of *A Portrait of the Artist as a Young Man*.

2 – Stanislaus Joyce said this epiphany was based on 'a memory of [Joyce's] reading of novels by Erckmann-Chatrian – *L'Invasion* at school, *L'Ami Fritz*, *Le Juif Polonais*, and others for himself – in which these collaborators do not seem to have produced the effect they desired' (*MBK* 57/75). Emile Erckmann and Louis G. C. A. Chatrian wrote a large number of works between 1847 and 1889 under the joint name Erckmann-Chatrian. They were especially noted for their descriptions of Alsatian peasant life.

5 – This scene presumably took place in Joyce's great-aunts' house on Usher's Island after the death of Mary Ellen Callanan, Joyce's second cousin who was the model for Mary Jane in 'The Dead' (*JJ* 84, 246).

6 – This is presumably the 'Epiphany of Hell' referred to in Joyce's plan for *Stephen Hero* (*Workshop of Daedalus*, p. 69).

8 – A dream epiphany in which Stanislaus Joyce felt that he 'inhabited the body of a dog' (*MBK* 126/136).

9 – In the summer of 1900 Joyce's father was employed to straighten out the voting lists in Mullingar, in the centre of Ireland, and he took James and some of the other children along. See also Epiphany 15. In *Stephen Hero* Joyce describes Stephen at Mullingar, but in *Portrait* he omitted the episode, preferring to confine Stephen's debates to his university circle (*JJ* 77–8).

11 – The figure referred to is Ibsen, who in the context of the epiphany in *Stephen Hero* has been the subject of a guessing game.

16 – Stanislaus described this dream epiphany as 'one of the first of the collection, perhaps made before we left Royal Terrace [October 1902]' (*MBK* 126/135).

17 – This epiphany refers to Joyce's 'The Day of the Rabblement', an essay condemning the parochialism of the Irish national theatre that was published in October 1901 along with an essay by his friend Francis Skeffington advocating equal status for women. (Skeffington later married Hanna Sheehy and changed his name to Sheehy Skeffington.) Maggie Sheehy is parodying the close of Joyce's essay: 'Elsewhere there are men who are worthy to carry on the tradition of the old master [Ibsen] who is dying in Christiania. He has already found his successor in the writer of *Michael Kramer* [Hauptmann], and the third minister will not be wanting when his hour comes. Even now that hour may be standing by the door.'

19 – Joyce's brother Georgie died on 9 March 1902. This scene was reworked to describe the death of Isabel in *Stephen Hero*.

20 – Another epiphany recalling the death of Georgie.

21 – Stanislaus remembered that this epiphany was written two or three months after the death of their mother (13 August 1903) (*MBK* 235/231).

22 – Another reference to the death of Joyce's brother Georgie.

23 – Joyce 'thought that by the boy in [this] dream-epiphany Georgie was intended' (*MBK* 136/144).

24 – The closing line, from the Vulgate Song of Solomon, is translated in the King James Version (1:13) as 'he shall lie all night betwixt my breasts'.

26 – As Stanislaus recalled, Joyce was 'invited to a dance at the Sheehys' to celebrate, I think, an engagement . . . To be able to go to the dance, Jim had to borrow a dress-suit from [Oliver St John] Gogarty, and although Gogarty was bulkier and there was some slight difference in height, Jim looked well in his borrowed finery. The dance was at least the occasion for an epiphany in which the girl in whose honour the dance was given figures anonymously'. Stanislaus surmised that the subject of this epiphany was the same girl who prompted 24 (*MBK* 256-7/250-1).

30 – This epiphany signals Stephen Dedalus's departure for Paris at the close of both *Stephen Hero* and *Portrait*.

31 – Stanislaus placed this epiphany in late 1903, as marking the end of Joyce's 'brief appearance in the garb of a "piping poet" ' (*MBK* 253/247).

33 – A 'fleeting memory of a Parisian scene' (*MBK* 254/248). This epiphany and the remaining seven were based on Joyce's experiences after his departure for Paris, and do not fall within the scope of *Stephen Hero* and *Portrait*.

34 – 'Alone in Paris my brother had felt the black shadow of the priest that had fallen between him and his mother fade away into a vague, troubled memory. She had come to him in a dream confused in his sleeping brain with the image of the Virgin Mother . . . The epiphany may have been suggested by a letter of my mother. In answering one of my brother's more desperate and disheartened outpourings she had spoken comfortingly of her love for him when he was a child. The sudden summons home [MOTHER DYING COME HOME FATHER] had come like the rude shock of reality . . . it left indelible traces on his soul' (*MBK* 229–30/226–7). In the 'Circe' episode of *Ulysses* the ghost of Stephen's mother says: 'Years and years I loved you, O, my son, my firstborn, when you lay in my womb.' (15.4203–4/581/516).

36 – A dream epiphany in which 'the greatest man in the world' is Ibsen (*MBK* 126/136).

37 – A memory of Joyce's return from Paris via Dieppe–Newhaven in April 1903 to be at the bedside of his dying mother.

40 – This epiphany reflects Joyce's ambivalent feelings towards his friend/enemy Oliver St John Gogarty, the model for Buck Mulligan in *Ulysses*. Rutland Square was a 'good' address, in contrast to the declining fortunes of the Joyce family.

In this sketch we have the only surviving example of Joyce's care in reworking the epiphanies.

A Portrait of the Artist

The text of 'A Portrait of the Artist' is taken from Joyce's holograph copy in Mabel Joyce's exercise book. Where this copy is illegible, due primarily to flaking of the first and last pages, the text has been supplemented, whenever possible, with the partial holograph copy made by Stanislaus Joyce around the time of his brother's own copy. The least satisfactory supplementary source is the typescript which Stanislaus probably had made late in 1927 or early in 1928, when his brother requested a copy of the essay to present to Sylvia Beach. All of these documents are reproduced in *The James Joyce Archive*, vol. 7 (New York, 1978), pp. 70–105.

Passages that Joyce crossed out as he used them in later works are set within angle brackets. Additions to the text from Stanislaus's manuscript and typescript are enclosed in square brackets. Undeciphered passages are indicated by ellipses. The diagonal lines setting off the passage on page 215 are Joyce's.

Only substantive variants have been noted.

1 – Joyce wrote an explanatory note to Sylvia Beach on the inside back cover of the notebook: 'Note, the foregoing pages are the first draft of an essay of *A Portrait of the Artist as a Young Man* and a sketch of the plot and characters, written (January 1904) in a copybook of my sister Mabel (b. 1896, d. 1911). The essay was written for a Dublin review *Dana* but refused insertion by the editors Mr W K Magee (John Eglinton) and Mr Frederick Ryan. | James Joyce | 20.1.1928 | Paris.' Added, in Beach's hand, 'gift from James Joyce to Sylvia Beach | 20.1.1928.' The letter that Joyce included with his MS is collected in *James Joyce's Letters to Sylvia Beach, 1921–1940*, ed. M. Banta and O. A. Silverman (Bloomington, 1987), p. 133. In the entry for 2 February 1904 of his *Complete Dublin Diary*, Stanislaus records the early history of this essay: 'He [Jim] has decided to turn his paper into a novel, and having come to that decision is just as glad, he says, that it was rejected . . . Jim is beginning his novel, as he usually begins such things, half in anger, to show that in writing about himself he has a subject of more interest than their aimless discussion. I suggested the title of the paper "A Portrait of the Artist" . . . It is to be almost autobiographical, and naturally as it comes from Jim, satirical . . .' (Ithaca, 1971, pp. 11–12).

2 – Joyce described *Finnegans Wake* to Jacques Mercanton in comparable terms: 'There is no past, no future; everything flows in an eternal present'

(Jacques Mercanton, 'The Hours of James Joyce', in *Portraits of the Artist in Exile*, ed. Willard Potts, New York, 1979, p. 207).

3 – Stephen provides Lynch with a more carefully phrased version of the concept in *Portrait*: 'Rhythm . . . is the first formal esthetic relation of part to part in any esthetic whole or of an esthetic whole to its part or parts or of any part to the esthetic whole of which it is a part' (206/187). Bloom echoes the definition in his sleepy Masonic murmur at the end of 'Circe': 'any part or parts, art or arts . . .' (*U* 15.4952/609/532).

4 – 'He thought of his own [fervid religiousness] spendthrift religiousness and airs of the cloister, he remembered having astonished a labourer in a wood near Malahide by an ecstasy of oriental posture' (*SH* 156/141). 'And he remembered an evening when he had dismounted from a borrowed creaking bicycle to pray to God in a wood near Malahide' (*P* 232/209–10).

5 – The sentence echoes several passages from John Henry Newman, *An Essay in Aid of a Grammar of Assent* (London, 1870), e.g. pp. 86, 208. Stephen quotes Newman's *Grammar* in *Portrait* (164/149).

6 – 'He had failed to understand that most marketable goodness which makes it possible to give comfortable assent to propositions without in the least ordering one's life in accordance with them and had failed to appreciate the digestive value of the sacraments' (*SH* 156/141).

7 – Cf. *SH* 177/159. Stephen prefers the 'mild', 'quaint' Saint Francis (*SH* 176/159) to the worldly Father Healy (*SH* 156–8/141–3) or the sensual Father Moran (*SH* 65–6/63). He confesses to an appropriately 'old and weary' priest in *Portrait* (143–5/132–3).

8 – 'Stephen's style of writing, . . . though it was over affectionate towards the antique and even the obsolete and too easily rhetorical, was remarkable for a certain crude originality of expression. He gave himself no great trouble to sustain the boldnesses which were expressed or implied in his essays. He threw them out as sudden defence-works while he was busy constructing the enigma of a manner' (*SH* 27/30). 'He was an enigmatic figure in the midst of his shivering society where he enjoyed a reputation' (*SH* 35/36). Stephen finds the speeches of Yeats's characters, Owen Aherne and Michael Robartes, 'like the enigmas of a disdainful Jesus; their morality was infrahuman or super-human . . .' (*SH* 178/160; cf. *SH* 112/103). See also the note following 'A Portrait of the Artist' in Mabel's notebook: 'Enigmatical Christ – enigmatical men counsel [connected?] with him' (Robert Scholes and Richard Kain, eds., *Workshop of Daedalus*, Evanston, 1965, p. 72).

9 – Cf. *SH* 29/32.

10 – Cf. *SH* 34/35.

11 – This playground scene is repeated in *SH* 34/35–6; *P* 8/8.

12 – Cf. *SH* 35/36. In his *Autobiography* Yeats recalls: 'During the quarrel over Parnell's grave a quotation from Goethe ran through the papers,

describing our Irish jealousy: "The Irish seem to me like a pack of hounds, always dragging down some noble stag" ' (New York, 1953, p. 190). Joyce adopts the simile in 'The Shade of Parnell': 'He [Parnell] went from county to county, from city to city, "like a hunted deer . . ." ' (CW 227). Joyce turns these antlers against Yeats (among others) in 'The Holy Office':

> I stand the self-doomed, unafraid,
> Unfellowed, friendless and alone,
> Indifferent as the herring-bone,
> Firm as the mountain-ridges where
> I flash my antlers on the air. (p. 99)

Stephen casts himself in Parnell's pose when the dog approaches him in 'Proteus': 'I just simply stood pale, silent, bayed about' (U 3.311/45/51). The antlered Dedalus is transfigured in 'Circe': '*Stephen and Bloom gaze in the mirror. The face of William Shakespeare, beardless, appears there, rigid in facial paralysis, crowned by the reflection of the reindeer antlered hatrack in the hall*' (U 15.3821–4/567/508). The quotation from Goethe may be found in Johann Eckermann, *Conversations with Goethe*: 'The Catholics, though they do not agree among themselves, will always unite against a Protestant. They are like a pack of hounds, who will be biting one another until a stag comes in view, when they all unite to run it down' (entry for 7 April 1829).

13 – In *A Midsummer Night's Dream* Theseus and Hippolyta plan to retreat to 'the mountain's top' where they can 'mark the musical confusion / Of hounds and echo in conjunction' (IV.i). Their subsequent encounter and conversation with the confused young lovers is suggested by Joyce's own '[lofty] diagnosis of the younglings'.

14 – Emile Zola (1840–1902). Stephen listens scornfully to Moynihan's inaugural address that alludes 'to the strange death of a French atheistic writer and [implies] that Emmanuel had chosen to revenge himself on the unhappy gentleman by privily tampering with his gas-stove' (SH 172/155). It is probable that Joyce had not read Zola when he wrote this essay. In a letter to Stanislaus dated 7 December 1906, he complains, 'I should like to read Zola but have not the heart to attack his twenty volume history of France' (L, II, 202).

15 – Father Healy agrees with McCann that 'Gladstone was the greatest man of the nineteenth century' (SH 157/142). Stephen overhears an anonymous student repeating a priest's judgement that 'the three greatest men in Europe were Gladstone, Bismarck . . . and our own Archbishop' (SH 74/70). Stephen's journal in *Portrait* also recalls the statesman: 'I was once at a diorama in Rotunda. At the end were pictures of big nobs. Among them William Ewart Gladstone, just then dead. Orchestra played, *O, Willie, we have missed you*. A race of clodhoppers!' (249/225). In 'Home Rule Comes of Age' (1907), Joyce accuses Gladstone of having 'completed the moral

assassination of Parnell with the help of the Irish bishops' (*CW* 193). See also the portrait of Gladstone in 'The Shade of Parnell' (1912) (*CW* 223–4).

16 – Cf. *SH* 172/155.

17 – 'On his side chastity, having been found a great inconvenience, had been quietly abandoned and the youth amused himself in the company of certain of his fellow-students among whom (as the fame went) wild living was not unknown' (*SH* 35/36).

18 – Thomas Davis (1814–45), Irish poet and Protestant barrister, was recruited to Daniel O'Connell's Repeal Association in 1841. With Gavan Duffy and John Blake Dillon, Davis founded the separatist journal, *The Nation*, and gathered about him the group of men known as 'Young Ireland' (Malcolm Brown, *The Politics of Irish Literature*, Seattle, 1972, p. 50). See also *CW* 177.

19 – Terence Bellew MacManus (?1823–61), one of the Young Irelanders transported for his part in the uprisings of 1848. He died in San Francisco and his body was brought back for burial in Dublin. Although thousands participated in the procession to the cemetery, Archbishop Cullen boycotted the funeral (Brown, *Politics*, pp. 115, 165–6). Mr Casey asks Dante in *Portrait*, 'didn't they dishonour the ashes of Terence Bellew MacManus?' (38/36).

20 – Paul Cullen (1803–78), Bishop of Armagh (1849), Archbishop of Dublin (1852), Cardinal (1852), was the first Irishman named to the college of Cardinals. He opposed the Fenians' advocacy of violence (Brown, *Politics*, pp. 158, 175). Mr Casey recalls Cardinal Cullen in *Portrait*, 'I forgot little old Paul Cullen! Another apple of God's eye!' (38/36). See also *SH* 173/155.

21 – Stephen takes *Othello* 'more seriously' than his fellow students at University; 'but at the same time he [is] amused to learn that the president had refused to allow two of the boarders to go to a performance . . . at the Gaiety Theatre on the ground that there were many coarse expressions in the play' (*SH* 29/32). Cf. *SH* 193/173.

22 – Simon Dedalus regales his son with stories of his happy youth in Cork as the two travel there to auction off the family property, but Stephen feels 'the world give the lie rudely to this fantasy' by 'the manner of his own dispossession' (*P* 87/81).

23 – In his moments of illumination 'by the lightnings of intuition', Stephen knows 'that the spirit of beauty had folded him round like a mantle and that in revery at least he had been acquainted with nobility' (*P* 177/160).

24 – In *Stephen Hero* it is Father Butt who suggests this remedy for Stephen (226/202), but it is 'Cranly's friend O'Neill Glynn' who becomes 'the clerk from Guinness', (*SH* 148, 117/134, 108). The possibility of a job at the brewery briefly reappears in *Finnegans Wake*: 'Ever thought about Guinness's?' (*FW* 299.30).

25 – Cf. *SH* 193/173. Stephen insists to Cranly that he does not merely seek a '*bonum simpliciter*: . . . lust, ambition, gluttony', but a '*bonum arduum*' (*SH* 179–80/162).

26 – Discussing the 'perfection of one's art' keeps Stephen 'away from such places of uncomely dalliance as the debating society and the warmly cushioned sodality' (*SH* 171/154).

27 – The sense of this sentence suggests that Joyce intended to write 'impossible' rather than 'possible'. This emendation is supported by the text of *Stephen Hero*: 'Impossible that he should find his soul's sufficient good in societies for the encouragement of thought among laymen, or any other than bodily solace in the warm sodality, in the company of those foolish and grotesque virginities!' (193/173–4). Stephen becomes a prefect of the sodality of the Virgin Mary in *Portrait* (104/97). The parable of the wise and foolish virgins is recounted in Matthew 25:1–13.

28 – Cf. *SH* 193–4/174.

29 – Joyce develops this 'arm-in-arm' walk into the scene between Stephen and Cranly (*SH* 137ff./125ff.; *P* 237ff./214ff.). Stephen's reading of Franciscan literature, particularly the 'legend of the mild heresiarch of Assisi', signals his heretical turn towards the mystical tradition, which culminates in his devotion to W. B. Yeats's stories of Michael Robartes and Owen Aherne (*SH* 176–7/159). Stephen imagines himself a 'heretic franciscan' as he talks with Emma Clery in *Portrait* (219–20/199).

30 – Cf. *SH* 179/161.

31 – *Poverello*: 'poor man, beggar'; 'Il Poverello d'Assisi' is idiomatic. The 'simple history' of the founder of the Franciscan order, Saint Francis of Assisi (?1182–1226), includes his conversion in his early twenties when he renounced his family's wealth. In the fervent exercise of his mission, he placed particular emphasis upon charity and humility.

32 – Joachim of Fiore (*c.* 1135–1202), theologian, prophet, founder and abbot of a monastery at San Giovanni in Fiore. In 1254 a Franciscan proclaimed Joachim's works to be the new gospel, superseding the Old and New Testaments. Joachim was named heresiarch by a Synod at Arles, *c.* 1260.

33 – Giordano Bruno of Nola (?1548–1600), Dominican theologian, was expelled from the Church and fled Rome (1576) to travel through Europe. He returned to Italy where he was arrested by the Inquisition (1592) for his cosmological theories and burned at the stake (1600). Joyce first refers to Bruno in the opening of his essay 'The Day of the Rabblement' (1901): 'No man, said the Nolan, can be a lover of the true or the good unless he abhors the multitude . . .' (*CW* 69 and n. 2). 'The Bruno Philosophy' (1903) contains Joyce's most extended discussion of Bruno's thought (*CW* 132–4). In *Stephen Hero* Father Artifoni tells Stephen that Bruno 'was a terrible heretic' to which Stephen responds, 'Yes . . . and he was terribly burned' (170/153; see also *P*

249/224). In *Finnegans Wake* he becomes, among other things, part of the composite 'Browne and Nolan' (Adaline Glasheen, *Third Census of Finnegans Wake*, Berkeley, 1977, pp. 40–1). See also *MBK* 145–6/152–4, and *L*, I, 226.

34 – Joyce uses the latinized name of Michael Sedziwoj (?1556–?1636), Polish or Moravian alchemist. Sedziwoj rescued the Scottish alchemist Alexander Seton from torture in prison and, when Seton died, married his wife and appropriated his alchemical secrets and his manuscripts. Sedziwoj declined to join the Rosicrucians, although they claimed him as a member. He is discussed in John Ferguson's *Bibliotheca Chemica* (Glasgow, 1906), II, pp. 368–9.

35 – Emmanuel Swedenborg (1688–1772), Swedish scientist, biblical scholar, and mystic who conceived of a complex system of correspondences between material and spiritual worlds. Joyce echoes the 'shapeless thoughts' of his *Heaven and Hell* (1758) in *Portrait* (224–5/203) and remarks in his essay on William Blake (1912) that 'Swedenborg . . . frequented all of the invisible worlds for several years' (*CW* 221).

36 – Saint John of the Cross (1542–91), Spanish mystic, poet, and theologian, reformer of the Carmelite order. Imprisoned by a conservative faction of Carmelites in 1577, he began writing poetry. Joyce names him 'one of the few idealist artists worthy to stand with Blake' (*CW* 221).

37 – A copy of *The Signature of All Things* (1622), by the German theologian, Jacob Boehme (1575–1624), is listed in an inventory of books in Joyce's Trieste library (Richard Ellmann, *The Consciousness of Joyce*, 1977, p. 102). Cf. Stephen on the strand in 'Proteus': 'Signatures of all things I am here to read' (*U* 3.2/37/42).

38 – Stephen imagines himself an alchemical 'priest of eternal imagination, transmuting the daily bread of experience into the radiant body of everliving life' (*P* 221/200). Cf. *FW* 185.35–6.

39 – Stephen meditates on the 'balance of the period' in *Portrait* (166–7/151–2).

40 – Stephen ties mother and Church together in *Stephen Hero* (137–43/125–30) and in *Portrait* (238–47/215–23) and presents a similar list of obstacles to Davin: 'nationality, language, religion' (*P* 203/184).

41 – For an illustration of the mystical geometry that Joyce mocks, see Mme Blavatsky, *Isis Unveiled* (1877, rpt. Wheaton, Illinois, 1972), II, pp. 269–70 and the diagrams following p. 258. Stanislaus describes his brother temporarily '[toying] with theosophy as a kind of interim religion', and notes that James 'read with serious intent expository works on theosophy by Madame Blavatsky' and others. Stanislaus's 'disrespectful transformation' of 'Blavatsky' into 'Bluefatsky (a name that suited her flabby, puckered face and puckered eyes that seemed to be peering through cigarette smoke)' perhaps explains the 'blue triangles' above (*MBK* 131/140).

42 – Buck Mulligan facetiously encourages Haines to write 'five lines of text and ten pages of notes about the folk and the fishgods of Dundrum' (*U* 1.365–6/12–13/19). The 'fish-god' is probably the Irish sea-god, Manannan MacLir. Joyce has augmented Manannan's fishy qualities by the time he appears in 'Circe': '*A cold seawind blows from his druid mouth. About his head writhe eels and and elvers. He is encrusted with weeds and shells. His right hand holds a bicycle pump. His left hand grasps a huge crayfish by its two talons*' (*U* 15.2263–6/510/475). Lady Gregory offers an extensive collection of legends about Manannan in her *Gods and Fighting Men* (London, 1904), part 1, book 4, chs. 8–15.

43 – Weldon Thornton points out that similar references to 'sacrificial butter' and 'dreamery creamery butter' in *Ulysses* are an 'ironic joining of AE's [George Russell's] interests in theosophy and dairying; one of the primary concerns of *The Irish Homestead*, which AE edited, was dairy management, and every issue had a section entitled 'Creamery Management' (*Allusions in Ulysses*, Chapel Hill, 1968, p. 156). In addition, Joyce had probably read the chapter – entitled 'Bewitched Butter' in W. B. Yeats, ed., *Fairy and Folk Tales of the Irish Peasantry* (London, 1888).

44 – Objecting to the 'burgher notion' of the public artist, Stephen tells his brother Maurice that 'isolation is the first principle of artistic economy' (*SH* 33/34).

45 – Cf. Stephen's morning walk in *Portrait*: 'The rainladen trees of the avenue evoked in him, as always, memories of the girls and women in the plays of Gerhart Hauptmann; and the memory of their pale sorrows and the fragrance falling from the wet branches mingled in a mood of quiet joy' (176/159). The diagonal lines after 'frailty of all things' and following 'singing passionately to the tide' below are Joyce's later delineations of the passage for use in *Portrait*.

46 – This scene is developed in *Portrait* (170–3/155–7). In Joyce's essay, the passage does not culminate in a vision of a 'delicate' girl 'without shame or wantonness' (*P* 171/156), but in memories of a prostitute's sexual embrace (cf. *P* 100–1/92–4). See also 'Tutto è Sciolto' (p. 55).

47 – Stephen joins his brother Maurice on the strand in *Stephen Hero*: 'At times Stephen would half clothe himself and cross to the shallow side of the Bull, where he would wander up and down looking at the children and the nurses' (230/205).

48 – The boy in 'Araby', alone in 'the upper part of the house', waiting to begin his journey to the bazaar, similarly declares his private joy: 'The high cold empty gloomy rooms liberated me and I went from room to room singing' (*D* 33/29).

49 – The phrase, from *Confessions* 7.12, is quoted again in *Ulysses* (7.842–4/142/143).

50 – Two lines of Joyce's holograph are largely obscured by flaking paper. Partial reconstructions are from Stanislaus's TS.

51 – Joyce's phrase describes changing, fading colours, and refers to a species of fish (*Coryphaena hippuris*) popularly called 'dolphin', 'which, when it is taken out of the water, or is dying, undergoes rapid changes of hue' (*OED*). In *Portrait* these 'lights' become 'emerald and black and russet and olive' seaweed (170/155). In the Nighttown version of Stephen's encounter with the feminine, '(*the lights change, glow, fade gold rosy violet*)' (*U* 15.4049–50/575/513). 'The Mime of Mick, Nick and the Maggies' (*FW* 11.i) revolves around a guessing game in which femininity and the colours of the rainbow are repeatedly associated (*L*, I, 295).

52 – Cf. Stephen's tributary 'Villanelle of the Temptress' (p. 72; *P* 217ff./196ff.).

53 – Stephen recalls his childhood romance with Emma Clery as he considers sending her a copy of his Villanelle (*P* 222–3/200–1).

54 – In *Ulysses* Stephen remembers his mother's 'phantasmal mirth' (1.263/10/16).

55 – In *Portrait* Stephen has 'awakened from a slumber of centuries' as he enters Nighttown (100/92).

56 – Following his vision of the bird-girl on the strand, Stephen echoes this rhapsody: 'A wild angel had appeared to him, the angel of mortal youth and beauty, an envoy from the fair courts of life . . .' (*P* 172/156).

57 – In Epiphany 25, the girls' umbrellas are 'upheld at cunning angles' (p. 185). The description is repeated in *Portrait* (216/196).

58 – This litany to the unnamed woman who is 'Lady' and prostitute is analogous to Stephen's 'Villanelle of the Temptress', at once sacramental and profane. The young Stephen understands phrases from the Litany of Our Lady – 'Tower of Ivory. House of Gold' – by thinking of Eileen's hands and long hair (*P* 42–3/39–40).

59 – In *Portrait* Stephen similarly adores the Virgin (116/107). Apple trees contribute to the benediction in his journal: 'O life! Dark stream of swirling bogwater on which appletrees have cast down their delicate flowers' (*P* 250/226). See also *Chamber Music*, VII (p. 19).

60 – Stephen's pure meals in *Portrait* consist of 'White pudding and eggs and sausages and cups of tea' (146/133).

61 – 'Tale' in this sentence means 'enumeration' or 'list' as well as 'narrative'.

62 – Stephen worries that his art owes 'its very delicacy to a physical decrepitude, itself the brand and sign of vulgar ardours' (*SH* 162/146). His face is 'to a certain extent the face of a debauchee' (*SH* 23/27).

63 – Cf. *SH* 162/146.

64 – Stephen complains to Madden: 'can you expect me to settle everything all at once?' (*SH* 56/54).

65 – Probably Lady Augusta Gregory (1852–1932), playwright, folklorist, translator, who helped establish the Irish Literary Theatre. Yeats and George Russell introduced her to Joyce in November 1902 (*JJ* 104). Joyce first (unsuccessfully) requested money from her in 1902, before leaving for Paris (*JJ* 107). He closes his 1902 letter to Lady Gregory in terms similar to those of this essay: 'All things are inconstant except the faith in the soul, which changes all things and fills their inconstancy with light. And though I seem to have been driven out of my country here as a misbeliever I have found no man yet with a faith like mine' (*L*, 1, 53).

66 – Probably Thomas Hughes Kelly (1865–1933), American banking heir, lay dignitary of the Catholic church, supporter of Irish nationalism. Kelly gave Padraic Colum a five-year scholarship for writing in 1903. Joyce met Kelly on 5 December 1903 and, hoping to start a literary newspaper with Francis Skeffington, unsuccessfully requested an advance of £2000 (*JJ* 140–1; see also *MBK* 42/61–2). In 'The Holy Office', Joyce recalls Padraic Colum as 'him who plays the ragged patch / To millionaires in Hazelhatch' (p. 98). Stephen declares his 'verses are to be numbered among the spiritual assets of the State' (*SH* 202/181).

67 – Stephen dismisses Aristotle as a critic of 'the "inexact" sciences' in *Stephen Hero* (186/167). He is more generous in *Portrait*, acknowledging his 'search for the essence of beauty amid the spectral words of Aristotle or Aquinas', although he has assembled 'only a garner of slender sentences from Aristotle's poetics and psychology . . .' (*P* 176/160; see also *SH* 77ff./73ff.; *P* 187/170; *P* 204ff./185ff.).

68 – God calls to Moses 'out of the midst of the bush' that 'burned with fire, and . . . was not consumed' (Exodus 3:2–4).

69 – A wry characterization of the nationalistic poetry of the Irish Renaissance, particularly the attempts by W. B. Yeats, Lady Gregory and others to invigorate their art with Irish folk tales involving the supernatural.

70 – In Joyce's holograph 'Many' is written above 'Few', which is crossed out.

71 – Lynch offers 'proof of . . . culture' in *Portrait* (204/185).

72 – In *Ulysses* Stephen numbers Buck Mulligan among the 'brood of mockers' (1.657/21/27).

73 – The notes Joyce made in late 1904 while living in Pola refer to John Francis Byrne as 'His Intensity' (Scholes and Kain, *Workshop*, p. 89; see also *Complete Dublin Diary*, p. 48). 'Their Intensities' may be the Catholic church or Sinn Feiners; a 'bullock' is a countrified lout and may also suggest the government of 'John Bull'. In the sixteenth century, 'bullock' was used as slang for a papal bull (*OED*).

74 – *nego*: 'I deny'; the opposite of *credo*, 'I believe.' Cf. Stephen's '*non serviam*' in 'Circe' (*U* 15.4228/582/517). Joyce's specific reference is probably to 'The Day of the Rabblement' (1901), where he discusses the temptation of

Irish artists to make 'terms with the rabblement' (*CW* 69) and defines himself as one of the isolated few who will carry on Ibsen's crusade for Truth (*CW* 72).

75 – In *Stephen Hero* the Pope presides over 'the season for glorified believers and fried atheists' and creates 'obscene, stinking hells' (232/207).

76 – Stephen derives temporary encouragement from his political vision in *Stephen Hero*: 'Indeed he felt the morning in his blood: he was aware of some movement already proceeding out in Europe. Of this last phrase he was fond for it seemed to him to unroll the measurable world before the feet of the islanders' (35/36).

77 – The left-wing Social Democrats in Germany had been fighting for power with increasing success since the 1870s.

78 – Giovanni Giolitti (1842–1928), one of the leaders of Italy's constitutional left, had been chosen to serve as Premier in 1903.

79 – Stephen, imagining an audience of Irish women, wonders how to 'hit their conscience or how cast his shadow over the imaginations of their daughters, before their squires begat upon them, that they might breed a race less ignoble than their own?' (*P* 238/215). Working on his lecture, 'Drama and Life', in *Stephen Hero*, he hopes 'that the students might need only the word to enkindle them towards liberty or that, at least, his trumpet-call might bring to his side a certain minority of the elect' (49/48).

80 – Scholes and Kain suggest that Joyce intended 'lightening' (*Workshop*, p. 68 n. 22).

81 – Stanislaus describes his brother's political temper in 1904: 'Jim boasts . . . of being modern. He calls himself a socialist but attaches himself to no school of socialism. He marks the uprooting of feudal principles' (*Complete Dublin Diary*, p. 54).

82 – *general paralysis of the insane*: 'a disease usually affecting persons near the prime of life, and characterised by a stage of mental excitement with exalted delusions, followed by dementia; it is accompanied by a varying amount of loss of muscular power' (*OED*). Don Gifford describes '*general paresis of the insane*' as 'the genteel medical term for syphilis of the central nervous system' and notes that 'among medical students in the British Isles g.p.i. was slang for eccentric' (*Ulysses Annotated*, 2nd edn, p. 15). 'Paralysis' characterizes Irish life in 'The Sisters' (*D* 9/7), and *Stephen Hero* (146/132). According to Buck Mulligan, Stephen is rumoured to suffer from this affliction: 'That fellow I was with in the Ship last night . . . says you have g.p.i. He's up in Dottyville with Connolly Norman. General paralysis of the insane!' (*U* 1.127–9/6/12).

Giacomo Joyce

The text of *Giacomo Joyce* is taken from the facsimile reproduction of Joyce's holograph manuscript, first published in Richard Ellmann's edition of *Giacomo Joyce* (New York: The Viking Press, London: Faber and Faber, 1968).

1 – For extended discussions of the identity of Joyce's student, see Helen Barolini, 'The Curious Case of Amalia Popper', and Richard Ellmann's response, *The New York Review of Books* (20 Nov. 1969), pp. 44–51.

2 – Mrs Bellingham wears furs and uses 'tortoishell quizzing-glasses' in 'Circe' (*U* 15.1026–7/465–6/448).

3 – Cf. Molly's 'Yes' concluding 'Penelope'.

4 – See 'A Portrait of the Artist', p. 282 n. 35.

5 – 'The Pseudo-Areopagite', or 'Pseudo-Dionysius' are names given to the Christian theologian whose mystical treatises and letters appeared in the early sixth century under the name of Dionysius the Areopagite. Paul converted Dionysius the Areopagite at Athens (Acts 17:34). Joyce discusses Dionysius' approach to 'divine obscurity' in his essay 'William Blake' (1912) (*CW* 222).

6 – Miguel de Molinos (1640–97), Spanish mystic who died in prison after being condemned by the Inquisition in 1687. Joyce mentions him in 'The Bruno Philosophy' (1903) (*CW* 134).

7 – See 'A Portrait of the Artist', p. 281 n. 32. Stephen quotes the *Vaticinia Pontificum* (Venice, 1589), a spurious edition attributed to Joachim, in 'Proteus' (3.112–14/39–40/45). Joyce had completed the first draft of this chapter just before leaving Trieste for Zurich in June 1915 (A. Walton Litz, *The Art of James Joyce*, London, 1961, p. 142). Cf. *SH* 176–7/159.

8 – The 'fourworded wavespeech' in 'Proteus' concludes similarly: 'spent, its speech ceases' (*U* 3.456–9/49/55).

9 – *Che coltura!*: 'What culture!'

10 – Stephen holds that 'Jews . . . are of all races the most given to intermarriage' (*U* 9.783–4/205/206).

11 – In *Portrait* Stephen admits that a 'girl he had glanced at' may possess 'the secret of her race' (220–1/199).

12 – Leopold Bloom, recalling his father's poisoned body, remembers 'yellow streaks on his face' (*U* 6.362–3/97/98/).

13 – Leopold Bloom remembers Molly's 'mawkish pulp' and 'soft' lips in 'Lestrygonians' (*U* 8.907–8, 909/176/176). Fritz Senn suggests that 'the whole

paragraph, interlarded with food terms, anticipates the technique and the vocabulary of the Lestrygonians chapter' ('Some Further Notes on *Giacomo Joyce*', *James Joyce Quarterly*, 5, 1968, p. 233).

14 – Joyce wrote of the same incident in 'A Flower Given to My Daughter' (p. 53), dated 'Trieste, 1913'. A 'frail pallor' characterizes Stephen's 'temptress' of the Villanelle (*P* 222–3/201).

15 – *Cinque servizi per cinque franchi*: 'Five favours for five francs.'

16 – Joyce returned to Trieste from Zurich in mid-October 1919, and may have consulted the *Giacomo Joyce* MS there when elaborating this paragraph in 'Oxen of the Sun' (*U* 14.1080–5/414/411). The 'fillyfoal' becomes 'Millicent [Bloom], the young' in the following paragraph (*U* 14.1101/414/411). Joyce began work on 'Oxen' in February 1920 and completed a first draft of the chapter in May 1920 (Litz, *Art of James Joyce*, p. 144).

17 – Stephen alludes to these lines from *Hamlet* (i.v) in *Ulysses* (15.3941/572/510).

18 – 'To lace up crisscrossed' is part of Bloom's punishment in 'Circe' (*U* 15.2815/529/487).

19 – In 'Lotus Eaters', a woman in 'high brown boots with laces dangling' and a 'wellturned foot' (*U* 5.117–18/74/75) commands Bloom's attention: 'Watch! Watch! Silk flash rich stockings white. Watch!' (*U* 5. /130/74/76).

20 – Modified from the conclusion of William Cowper's 'John Gilpin' (1782): 'And when he next doth ride abroad / May I be there to see!'

21 – *Mio padre*: 'My father'; *Unde derivatur?*: 'From where does she come?; *Mia figlia ha una grandissima ammirazione per il suo maestro inglese*: 'My daughter has enormous admiration for her teacher who is English.'

22 – Saint Ignatius of Loyola (1491–1556) founded the Jesuit order in 1540. Stephen invokes Loyola's aid before presenting his theory of *Hamlet* in 'Scylla and Charybdis' (*U* 9.163/188/188).

23 – Stephen's mother bears a 'ghostcandle to light her agony' (*U* 1.274/10/16), and he later envisages the 'Bridebed, childbed, bed of death, ghostcandled' (*U* 3.396/47–8/53).

24 – Ada Hirsch Meissel, wife of Filippo Meissel, committed suicide on 20 October 1911. Joyce visited her grave with her widower in the autumn of 1912 (*JJ* 345).

25 – Emma Clery allows Stephen to help her into her jacket: 'she allowed his hands to rest for a moment against the warm flesh of her shoulders' (*SH* 47/47).

26 – Molly asks Leopold to 'Give us a touch, Poldy' (*U* 6.80–1/89/90). Laertes, in his duel with Hamlet, acknowledges a hit: 'A touch, a touch' (v.ii).

27 – *Aber das ist eine Schweinerei!*: 'but that is a dirty trick!'

28 – Mrs Mervyn Talboys *stamps her jingling spurs in a sudden paroxysm of fury* at 'the pigeonlivered cur', Bloom (*U* 15.1081, 82/467/449). Molly, 'in

disdain', is 'plump as a pampered pouter pigeon' (*U* 15.352–3/441/433). Stephen likens the girl on the strand in *Portrait* to a 'strange and beautiful seabird' and a 'darkplumaged dove' (171/155, 156).

29 – From a nursery rhyme that accompanies a child being ridden on an adult's knee. In the 'Proteus' episode Stephen thinks of a corpse 'bobbing a pace a pace a porpoise landward' (*U* 3.473/50/55). Later Bello Cohen, riding Bloom, cries 'The lady goes a pace a pace' (*U* 15.2947/534/490).

30 – Joyce recasts this passage (beginning with 'Trieste is waking') as a description of Paris in 'Proteus' (*U* 3.209–15/42/48). See also Epiphany 33 (p. 193).

31 – Stephen's journal records 'the sound of hoofs upon the road' (*P* 251/226).

32 – Joyce probably alludes to the moment in Ibsen's play when Hedda Gabler's former companion, Ejlert Lövborg, returns to find Hedda married. Once the two are alone, Lövborg recalls their past intimacy while denying Hedda's recent marriage to Jörgen Tesman, pointedly calling her 'Hedda Gabler' (Act II).

33 – Boylan buys 'ripe shamefaced peaches' before he visits Molly (*U* 10.305–6/227/226).

34 – Dilly Dedalus, watching the viceregal procession, sees the carriage pass, its 'wheelspokes spinning in the glare' (*U* 10.1228–9/253/252).

35 – *Summa contra Gentiles* (*c.* 1260): An exposition of arguments against the gentiles – heretics and nonbelievers – by Saint Thomas Aquinas (*c.* 1225–74), Italian Dominican theologian.

36 – Ettore Albini (1869–1954), music critic who wrote for the Roman socialist newspaper *Avanti!* (rather than for the Turin daily, *Il Secolo*), was expelled on 17 December 1911 from a performance in La Scala because he failed to stand when the 'Marcia Reale', anthem of the Kingdom of Italy, was played. The concert was a benefit for the Italian Red Cross and the families of soldiers killed or wounded in Libya, where Italy was fighting the Turks. Albini was repeatedly jailed or deported for his opposition to the monarchy, to fascism, and to nationalism.

37 – This remark, applied to Jews, is attributed to J. J. O'Molloy in *Ulysses* (12.1630/337/335).

38 – The phrase is from the Litany of the Blessed Virgin. 'Prudence' means 'wisdom' in the Litany; Joyce's secular application evokes the modern connotation of 'circumspect conduct'.

39 – This scene resembles Gerty Macdowell's exposure in 'Nausicaa' (*U* 13.695–9, 724–33/365–6/363–4). The wax model Bloom confesses he 'visited daily' wears 'cobweb hose' (*U* 15.2818/529/487).

40 – In good Triestine, *Se Pol?* and in Italian, *Si può?*: 'Is it permitted?'; 'May I?' The expression, suitable for a servant asking to enter a room, is used by the

buffoon Tonio as he begins his Prologue to Ruggiero Leoncavallo's *Pagliacci* (1892).

41 – Like many Renaissance composers, English lutanist and composer John Dowland (?1563–1626) wrote a 'Loth to Depart' – a song declaring the lover's reluctance to leave his beloved. In *Portrait* Stephen imagines himself playing 'a dainty song of the Elizabethans, a sad and sweet loth to depart' (219/198; see also *SH* 155/140). There is no record of the original words to Dowland's version (*The Collected Lute Music of John Dowland*, transcr. and ed. Diana Poulton and Basil Lam, London, 1978), pp. 212–17 and 332 n. 69. The people of Dalkey declare their town Dowland's birthplace (W. H. Grattan Flood, 'New Facts about John Dowland', *Gentleman's Magazine*, 301 (1906), pp. 287–91), a claim that Joyce knew (*L*, III, 449 and n. 4).

42 – This passage, from 'Here, opening from the darkness of desire' to 'clip and clip again', is recast in *Portrait* (233/210).

43 – See above, n. 30.

44 – *quia frigus erat*: 'because it was cold'. The phrase comes from the Gospel According to St John. Peter, having just denied his association with Jesus, warms himself at a fire outside Caiaphas's courtyard while Annas interrogates Jesus within. Peter stands with Caiaphas's men: 'And the servants and officers stood there, who had made a fire of coals; for it was cold . . .' (18:18).

45 – The prostration of the ministers and the reading from Hosea 6:1–6 begin the Good Friday Mass. The sixth chapter of Hosea opens: 'Come, and let us return unto the Lord: for he hath torn, and he will heal us; he hath smitten, and he will bind us up.' Stephen discusses the service at some length in *Stephen Hero*, obviously identifying himself with Christ: 'Jesus has no friend on Good Friday. . . . [He is] something between Socrates and a Gnostic Christ – A Christ of the Dark Ages' who is 'on strange terms with that father of his' (116–17/107). Vicki Mahaffey points out that 'in 1914 Good Friday again fell on April 10, as it had eleven years earlier' when Joyce attended the *Tenebrae* service at Notre Dame 'a few hours before he learned that his mother was dying' ('*Giacomo Joyce*', in *A Companion to Joyce Studies*, ed. Z. Bowen and J. F. Carens, Westport, 1984, pp. 399, 417 n. 23). After a provocative encounter with Emma, Stephen walks, 'humming to himself the chant of the Good Friday Gospel' (*SH* 189/170). Stanislaus describes James's profoundly emotional response to the Good Friday Mass (*MBK* 105/117–18).

46 – Images in this sentence are echoed, with different implications, in 'Nightpiece', dated 'Trieste, 1915' (p. 59).

47 – The 'sorrowful' mysteries of the Blessed Virgin, contemplated in the second decade of the Rosary, include the Crucifixion. See also *P* 148/135.

48 – As he is led in procession to his Crucifixion, Jesus admonishes the lamenting women: 'Daughters of Jerusalem, weep not for me' (Luke 23:28). In 'Circe', Zoe quotes this verse in Hebrew (*U* 15.1333–4/477/454).

49 – Joyce lectured on *Hamlet* at the Università del Popolo from November 1912 until February 1913 (William Quillian, 'Shakespeare in Trieste: Joyce's 1912 *Hamlet* Lectures', *James Joyce Quarterly*, 12, 1974–5, p. 16 n. 2.

50 – In his discourse on Shakespeare, Stephen declares 'The images of other males of his blood will repel him. He will see in them grotesque attempts of nature to foretell or to repeat himself' (*U* 9.433–5/195–6/196).

51 – Polonius, observing that Hamlet sits by Ophelia rather than his mother for the performance of the 'Mousetrap', asks Claudius: 'Do you mark that?' (III.ii).

52 – Stephen imagines Dilly drowning and carrying him with her in her 'lank coils of seaweed hair' (*U* 10.876/243/242). In Joyce's notes to *Exiles*, hair is 'the softly growing symbol of [Bertha's] girlhood. . . . A proud and shy instinct turns her mind away from the loosening of her bound-up hair' (*E* 119, 120). The 'hell reserved for [Stephen's] sins' in *Portrait* contains 'clots and coils of solid excrement' and 'Goatish creatures' that move in 'slow circles' (137–8/126). See also n. 81, below.

53 – Vicki Mahaffey notes that this image 'may have been suggested by one of Rossetti's illustrations in the Italian version of *La Vita Nuova* that Joyce owned in Trieste, entitled "Beatrice nega il saluto a Dante" ' ('*Giacomo Joyce*', pp. 408–9 and 419 n. 40).

54 – The name not only evokes Dante's Beatrice and Shelley's Beatrice Cenci (whose brother's name is Giacomo), but is employed again by Joyce for Beatrice Justice in *Exiles*.

55 – The quotation is from Beatrice's death speech at the end of Shelley's *The Cenci* (v.iv.159–61).

56 – Vicki Mahaffey suggests that this simile echoes Orsino's description of the helpless Beatrice in *The Cenci*: 'I were a fool, not less than if a panther / Were panic-stricken by the antelope's eye, / If she escape me' (1.ii.88–90; '*Giacomo Joyce*', p. 410).

57 – In 'Proteus' Stephen thinks of 'the virgin at Hodges Figgis' window', who 'lives in Leeson park with a grief and kickshaws, a lady of letters' (*U* 3.426–7, 429–30/48/54).

58 – *Parlerò colla mamma*: 'I will speak with mother.'

59 – Bloom mocks the cat in 'Calypso' for being 'afraid of the chookchooks [chickens]' (*U* 4.30–1/55/57).

60 – *Loggione*: the top gallery in an opera house.

61 – In *Portrait* Stephen recalls 'an obscene scrawl which he had read on the oozing wall of a urinal' (100/92).

62 – The prostitute who accosts Stephen in *Stephen Hero* gives off 'an odour of ancient sweats' (189/170). Zoe leads Bloom 'by the odour of her armpits, . . . the lion reek of all the male brutes that have possessed her' (*U* 15.2015, 2017/501/469).

63 – Bloom embellishes *Sweets of Sin* by imagining 'melting breast ointments' and 'Armpits' oniony sweat' (*U* 10.621, 622/236/235).

64 – *mastick water*: a solution made with 'a gum or resin which exudes from the bark of *Pistacia lentiscus* and some other trees' (*OED*).

65 – *opoponax*: a sweet, heavy perfume made from the resin of *Opoponax chironium*, once imported from Turkey and the East Indies; 'Molly likes opoponax' (*U* 13.1010/374/372).

66 – Vicki Mahaffey notes that Joyce echoes Whitman, who likens grass to 'the beautiful uncut hair of graves' ('Song of Myself' 6.110; '*Giacomo Joyce*', p. 397).

67 – In *Portrait* Cranly's 'epitaph for all dead friendships' sinks into Stephen's mind 'like a stone through a quagmire' (195/177).

68 – Joyce corrects the spelling and recasts the phrase in *Portrait*: 'Her eyes, dark and with a look of languor, were opening to his eyes' (223/201).

69 – Stephen, in his first encounter with a prostitute, feels 'her softly parting lips. They pressed upon his brain as upon his lips' (*P* 101/94). The erotic turns gothic in *Ulysses* when Stephen confronts his mother. She is clothed '*in leper grey, . . . her face worn and noseless . . . Her hair is scant and lank*' (15.4157–60/579/515). She '*[breathes] upon him softly her breath of wetted ashes*' (*U* 15.4182/580/516).

70 – Zoe's '*odalisk lips*' are '*lusciously smeared*' (*U* 15.1332/477/454).

71 – Stephen's soul dissolves, 'flooding all the heavens', after he sees the bird-girl (*P* 172/157). The same imaginary possession occurs later in *Portrait*: 'Her nakedness yielded to him, radiant, warm, odorous and lavishlimbed, enfolded him like a shining cloud, enfolded him like water with a liquid life: and like a cloud of vapour or like waters circumfluent in space the liquid letters of speech, symbols of the element of mystery, flowed forth over his brain' (223/201). Bertha collaborates with Robert's erotic dream in the last act of *Exiles*:

ROBERT, *catching her hands*: Bertha! What happened last night? What is the truth that I am to tell? *He gazes earnestly into her eyes*. Were you mine in that sacred night of love? Or have I dreamed it?

BERTHA, *Smiles faintly*: Remember your dream of me. You dreamed that I was yours last night.

ROBERT: And that is the truth – a dream? That is what I am to tell?

BERTHA: Yes.

ROBERT, *kisses both her hands*: Bertha! *In a softer voice*. In all my life only that dream is real. I forget the rest. *He kisses her hands again*. And now I can tell him the truth. Call him.   (*E* 106)

72 – Baron Ambrogio Ralli (1878–1938), a prominent Triestine and one of Joyce's pupils, had a palazzo in Piazza Scorcola.

73 – Bello's is a '*hard basilisk stare*' (*U* 15.2835/530/487). Stephen imagines a priest 'clutching a monstrance, basiliskeyed' (*U* 3.115–16/40/45).

74 – *E col suo vedere attosca l'uomo quando lo vede*: 'and with his sight he destroys the man who sees him.' Quoted from Brunetto Latini (?1210–?1295), *Il Tesoro*, trans. Bono Giamboni from Latini's French text, ed. P. Chabaille, 4 vols., Bologna, 1877, II, p. 138. In *Ulysses* Joyce makes the Italian more colloquial: 'Stephen withstood the bane of miscreant eyes glinting stern under wrinkled brows. A basilisk. *E quando vede l'umo l'attosca*. Messer Brunetto, I thank thee for the word' (9.373–5/194/194). Cf. 'a jet of liquorish venom' in the following section.

75 – This section resembles Bloom's dream, with its 'Open hallway. Street of harlots . . . Red carpet spread' (*U* 3.365–6, 369/47/52).

76 – 'The Bawd' spits her 'jet of venom' at Stephen and Lynch in 'Circe' (*U* 15.86/431/427).

77 – See 'A Portrait of the Artist', n. 79.

78 – The phrase recalls Stephen's figure of Irish womanhood taken from Davin's story in *Portrait*: 'a type of her race and his own, a batlike soul waking to the consciousness of itself in darkness . . .' (183/166). See above, n. 11.

79 – Stephen's mother initially utters a 'silent word' to her son, who has just danced himself into a trance where 'Stars all around suns turn roundabout' (*U* 15.4161, 4152–3/579/515). See also n. 88, below, and Joyce's accompanying text.

80 – Stephen pleads with his mother's ghost for wisdom: 'Tell me the word, mother, if you know now. The word known to all men' (*U* 15.4192–3/581/516).

81 – Milly Bloom appears in 'Oxen of the Sun' with a gossamer veil flowing 'about her starborn flesh, . . . winding, coiling . . . [in] a myriad metamorphoses of symbol' (*U* 14.1104–8/414/411). The woman's ominous approach here is reminiscent of the 'figure' that comes to Stephen in 'the winding darkness of sleep' (*P* 99/91). See also n. 52, above.

82 – Both Vicki Mahaffey ('*Giacomo Joyce*', 417 n. 25) and Matthew Hodgart ('A Portrait of the Artist as a Middle-Aged Adulterer', *New York Review of Books*, 29 Feb. 1968, p. 3) suggest that this passage (from 'A soft crumpled peagreen cover' to 'Jim, love!') was written after the rest of *Giacomo Joyce* was complete.

83 – Father Dolan's pandybat makes Stephen's 'trembling hand crumple together like a leaf in the fire' (*P* 50/46). Fleming squeezes 'his hands under his armpits' after his pandying (*P*49/45). See also nn. 62, 63.

84 – Stephen has Eve similarly ravished in 'Scylla and Charybdis': 'A snake coils her, fang in's kiss' (*U* 9.541/199/199), and he imagines his own 'bestial part' in the same terms: 'His soul sickened at the thought of a torpid snaky life feeding itself out of the tender marrow of his life and fattening upon the slime of lust' (*P* 139, 140/128).

85 – Stephen talks to Bloom about this song in *Ulysses*: 'Exquisite variations he was now describing on an air *Youth here has End* by Jans Pieter Sweelinck, a Dutchman of Amsterdam where the frows come from' (16.1810–12/663/583).

86 – Stephen, his mother's 'claws' in his heart, also ages, 'his features drawn grey and old' (*U* 15.4223/582/517).

87 – These words are repeated in *Exiles*, following Richard's suggestion to Beatrice that she is the subject of 'a book of sketches', which Adaline Glasheen suggests is *Giacomo Joyce* ('Review Article: *Giacomo Joyce*', *Wake Newslitter*, 5, 1968, pp. 43–4):

BEATRICE . . . : Why do you think I come here?

RICHARD: Why? Many reasons . . . Perhaps you feel that some new thing is gathering in my brain; perhaps you feel that you should know it. Is that the reason?

BEATRICE: No.

RICHARD: Why, then?

BEATRICE: Otherwise I could not see you. . . .

RICHARD . . . : Otherwise you could not see me?   (*E* 18–19)

In the third act, Richard quotes Beatrice to herself:

RICHARD . . . : There are demons . . . out there. I heard them jabbering since dawn. . . . The isle is full of voices. Yours also. *Otherwise I could not see you*, it said. And her [Bertha's] voice. But, I assure you, they are all demons.

BEATRICE: [Offers a '*stammering*' explanation of her presence.]

RICHARD . . . : My dear Miss Justice, you told me yesterday, I think, why you came here and I never forget anything.   (*E* 98–9)

88 – Stephen's drunken dance in 'Circe' leaves him reeling, almost annihilated: '*Red rails fly spacewards. Stars all around suns turn roundabout. Bright midges dance on walls. He stops dead*' (*U* 15.4152–4/579/515). 'Her voice' becomes the voice of Stephen's mother. See also n. 79, above, and Joyce's accompanying text.

89 – *Non hunc sed Barabbam!*: The priests and the crowd tell Pilate to pardon 'Not this man [Jesus] but Barabbas!' (Luke 23:18).

90 – See the coffin/piano in 'Sirens' (*U* 11.291–2/263/262); the 'pianola coffin' in 'Circe' (*U* 15.3674/561/505); the 'closed coffin' that is Molly's piano (*U* 17.1303/706/627).

91 – '*Stephen stands at the pianola on which sprawl his hat and ashplant*' (*U* 15.2071–2/503/470).

92 – 'Stephen looked down on a wide headless caubeen, hung on his ashplanthandle over his knee. My casque and sword' (*U* 9.295–6/192/192).

93 – Vicki Mahaffey points out the allusion to Hester Prynne's epitaph, which concludes Hawthorne's *The Scarlet Letter*: 'ON A FIELD SABLE, THE LETTER A, GULES' ('*Giacomo Joyce*', p. 411).

Index of Titles and First Lines

(This index includes only the poetry. Titles are set in italic).

A bard once in lakelapt Sirmione, 124
A birdless heaven, seadusk, one lone star, 55
A Flower Given to My Daughter, 53
After the tribulation of dark strife, 76
Again, 63
A Goldschmidt swam in a Kriegsverein, 119
A holy Hegelian Kettle, 110
Aiutami dunque, O Musa, nitidissima Calligraphia, 148
Alas, how sad the lover's lot, 89
All day I hear the noise of waters, 47
Alone, 60
A Memory of the Players in a Mirror at Midnight, 61
And I have sat amid the turbulent crowd, 80
And I shall have no peace there for Joyce comes more and more, 127
And now is come the war, the war, 116
À Pierre de Lanux, 142
A Portrait of the Artist as an Ancient Mariner, 143
A Prayer, 63
Are you not weary of ardent ways, 72
As I was going to Joyce Saint James', 141
At that hour when all things have repose, 15
A voice that sings, 74

Bahnhofstrasse, 62
Because your voice was at my side, 29
Be not sad because all men, 31
Bid adieu, adieu, adieu, 23
Bis Dat Qui Cito Dat, 126
Bran! Bran! the baker's ban, 130
Bright cap and streamers, 22
Brighter than glass Bandusian spring, 71
Buried Alive, 138
Buy a book in brown paper, 139

C'era una volta, una bella bambina, 114
Come-all-ye, 149
Come all you lairds and ladies and listen to my lay! 149
Come out to where the youth is met, 94
Crossing to the Coast, 137

Dear heart, why will you use me so, 41
Dear, I am asking a favour, 112
Dear quick, whose conscience buried deep, 145
Discarded, broken in two, 86
D. L. G., 119
Don't talk of Congo Stanley, 137
Dooleysprudence, 120

Ecce Puer, 67
Epilogue to Ibsen's 'Ghosts', 145
E. P. is fond of an extra inch, 135
Et Tu, Healy, 71

Father O'Ford, 138
Flood, 58
Flower to flower knits, 85
For he's a jolly queer fellow, 135
Frail the white rose and frail are, 53
Fréderic's Duck, 129
From dewy dreams, my soul, arise, 27

Gas from a Burner, 103
Gaunt in gloom, 59
Gentle lady, do not sing, 40
Gladly above, 75
Go ca'canny with the cognac, 139
G. O'Donnell, 109
Goldbrown upon the sated flood, 58
Goodbye, Zurich, I must leave you, 147
Gorse-flower makes but sorry dining, 80
Go seek her out all courteously, 25

Hands that soothe my burning eyes, 82
Have you heard of one Humpty Dumpty, 145
Have you heard of the admiral, Togo, 111
He travels after a winter sun, 51

He who hath glory lost, nor hath, 33
Hue's Hue? or Dalton's Dilemma, 137
Humptydump Dublin squeaks through his norse, 139

If any told the blue ones that, 113
I hear an army charging upon the land, 48
I heard their young hearts crying, 52
I intone the high anthem, 84
I met with an ancient scribelleer, 143
I never thought a fountain pen, 129
In the dark pine-wood, 32
In the soft nightfall, 86
I only ask you to give me your fair hands, 73
I said: I will go down to where, 92
I saw at Miss Beach's when midday was shining, 130
Is it dreadfully necessary, 133
I would in that sweet bosom be, 18

Jimmy Joyce, Jimmy Joyce, where have you been, 128
John Eglinton, my Jo, John, 111

Ladies and gents, you are here assembled, 103
Lament for the Yeomen, 116
La scintille de l'allumette, 73
L. B. lugubriously still treads the press of pain, 136
Lean out of the window, 17
Le bon repos, 148
Let us fling to the winds all moping and madness, 82
Lightly come or lightly go, 37
Lord, thou knowest my misery, 78
Love came to us in time gone by, 42
Love that I can give you, lady, 77

Man dear, did you never hear of buxom Molly Bloom at all, 131
My cot alas that dear old shady home, 71
My dove, my beautiful one, 26
My love is in a light attire, 19
Myself unto myself will give, 97

New Tipperary, 123
Nightpiece, 59
Now a whisper . . . now a gale, 82

Now have I fed and eaten up the rose, 138
Now let awhile my messmates be, 118
Now, O now, in this brown land, 45
Now Wallace he heard that Fréderic's was the dearest place to dine, 129

O cool is the valley now, 28
O Father O'Ford you've a masterful way with you, 138
Of cool sweet dew and radiance mild, 57
O fons Bandusiae, 71
Of spinach and gammon, 125
Of that so sweet imprisonment, 34
Of the dark past, 67
Of thy dark life, without a love, without a friend, 84
Oh! Budgeon, boozer, bard, and canvas dauber, 124
O, it is cold and still – alas! –, 90
O, it was out by Donnycarney, 43
O, Mr Poe, 126
On the Beach at Fontana, 56
O, queen, do on thy cloak, 83
O Sweetheart, hear you, 30
O, there are two brothers, the Fays, 113

Pennipomes Twoguineaseach, 144
P. J. T., 131
Poor little Georgie, the son of a lackey, 109
Post Ulixem Scriptum, 131
Pour la Rime Seulement, 142
Pour Ulysse IX, 136

Rain has fallen all the day, 44
Rain on Rahoon falls softly, softly falling, 54
'Requiem eternam dona ei, Domine', 83
Rosy Brook he bought a book, 130
Rouen is the rainiest place getting, 134

Say, ain't this success fool author, 136
Scalding tears shall not avail, 74
Scheveningen, 1927, 136
She is at peace where she is sleeping, 91
She Weeps Over Rahoon, 54
Silently she's combing, 36
Simples, 57

Sing a song of shillings, 144
Sleep now, O sleep now, 46
Solomon, 118
Some are comely and some are sour, 85
Stephen's Green, 140
Strings in the earth and air, 13

That I am feeble, that my feet, 81
The clinic was a patched one, 133
The eyes that mock me sign the way, 62
The flower I gave rejected lies, 114
The grieving soul. But no grief is thine, 81
The Holy Office, 97
The moon's greygolden meshes make, 60
The pig's in the barley, 125
The press and the public misled me, 128
There is a clean climber called Sykes, 117
There is a weird poet called Russell, 110
There is a young gallant named Sax, 115
There once was a Celtic librarian, 112
There once was an author named Wells, 118
There once was a lounger named Stephen, 117
There's a coughmixture scopolamine, 135
There's a donor of lavish largesse, 117
There's a funny facepainter dubbed Tuohy, 131
There's a genial young poetriarch Euge, 145
There's a George of the Georges named David, 119
There's a hairyfaced Moslem named Simon, 118
There's a maevusmarked maggot called Murphy, 151
There's a monarch who knows no repose, 115
There's an anthropoid consul called Bennett, 122
There was an old lady named Gregory, 109
There was a young priest named Delaney, 110
The Right Heart in the Wrong Place, 125
The Right Man in the Wrong Place, 125
The Sorrow of Love, 113
The twilight turns from amethyst, 14
The wind stood up and gave a shout, 140
They mouth love's language. Gnash, 61
This heart that flutters near my heart, 35
Though I thy Mithridates were, 39
Though there is no resurrection from the past, 79

Though we are leaving youth behind, 93
Thou leanest to the shell of night, 38
Thunders and sweeps along, 79
Tilly, 51
To Budgeon, raughty tinker, 124
Told sublimely in the language, 76
To Mrs H. G. who complained that her visitors kept late hours, 139
Troppa Grazia, Sant' Antonio!, 135
Tutto è Sciolto, 55

Up to rheumy Zurich came an Irishman one day, 123

Watching the Needleboats at San Sabba, 52
We will leave the village behind, 75
What colour's Jew Joyce when he's rude and grim both, 137
What counsel has the hooded moon, 24
When the shy star goes forth in heaven, 16
Where none murmureth, 78
Who goes amid the green wood, 20
Who is Sylvia, what is she, 127
Who is the man when all the gallant nations run to war, 120
Winds of May, that dance on the sea, 21
Wind thine arms round me, woman of sorcery, 77
Wind whines and whines the shingle, 56

Yanks who hae wi' Wallace read, 126
Yea, for this love of mine, 75